I 0505287

AI VAMPIRE COLORING BOOK

Hey there, I'm Jeremy Hubert Burt. I was feeling inspired and decided to use a prompt to create some 3D coloring book pages. The prompt I used was:

"Design an exhilarating coloring book page featuring a captivating ancient female vampire monster. Against a pristine white background, use bold black lines to illustrate the character's mysterious and alluring features, creating a sense of intrigue and excitement. wearing white clothes. sharp teeth. fangs. drinking blood. bat man. ugly. horror tone. ancient world.

Create a dark and atmospheric environment that complements the vampire monster with fangs character, immersing the viewer in a world of supernatural power. The background designs should evoke a sense of enchantment and suspense, capturing the imagination.

Outline the character with bold black lines, clearly defining the boundaries for coloring. This empowers enthusiasts to bring the vampire game character to life using their own creativity and imagination, leveraging the striking contrast of black and white.

The coloring book page promises an enthralling journey into the world of the vampire character. It invites individuals to engage in the art of coloring, providing a thrilling sense of relaxation and stress relief. Embrace the captivating essence of the character amidst the timeless contrast of black and white."

After creating the design, I decided to edit the levels in GIMP in greyscale image mode to give it that extra touch of depth and detail. The whole process only took me a day, and I'm really happy with the results. I even published the pages using the Sqribble ebook maker, which was super easy to use. Check out the link if you want to Publish Your eBook: https://bit.ly/3nVzjvK.

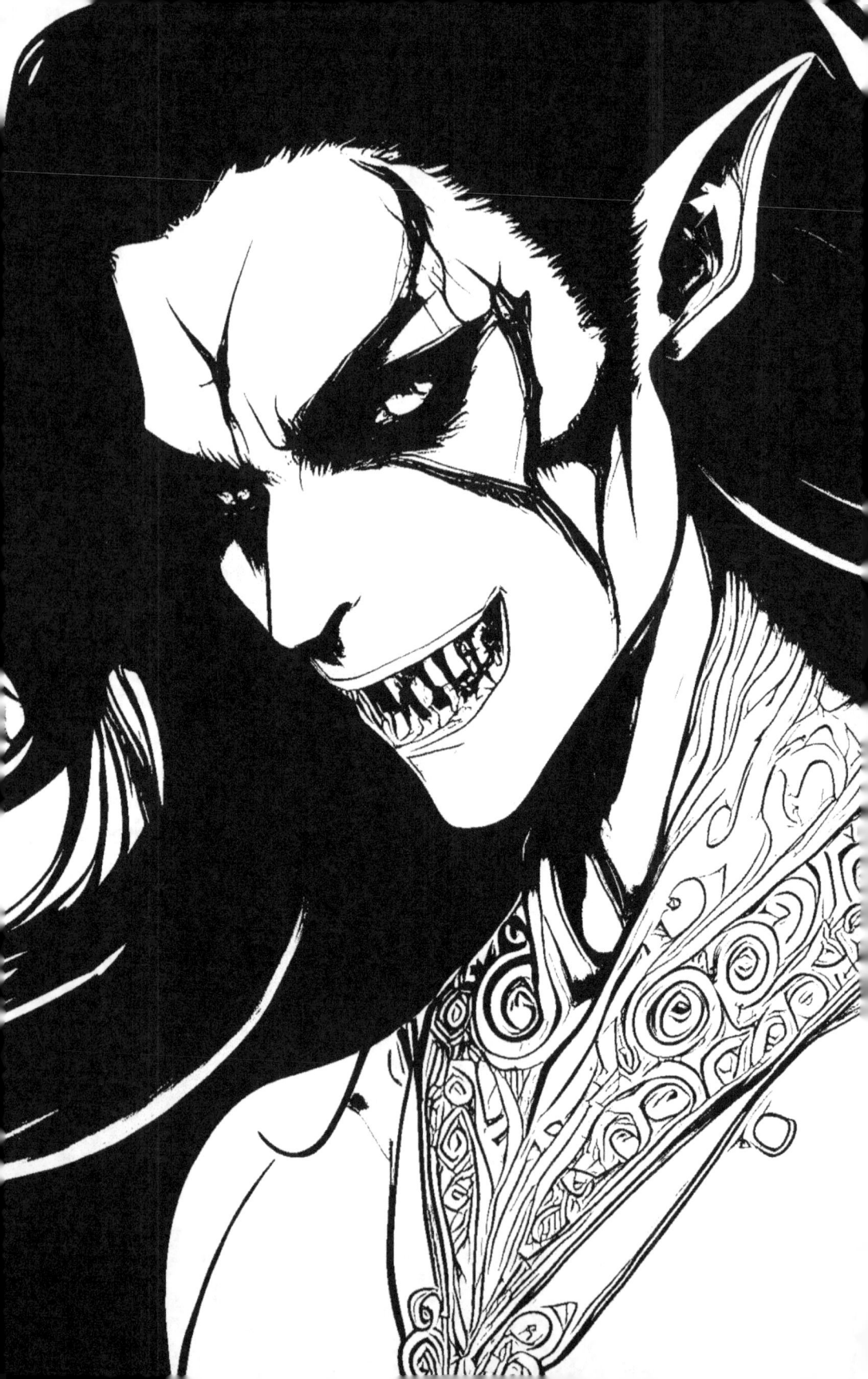

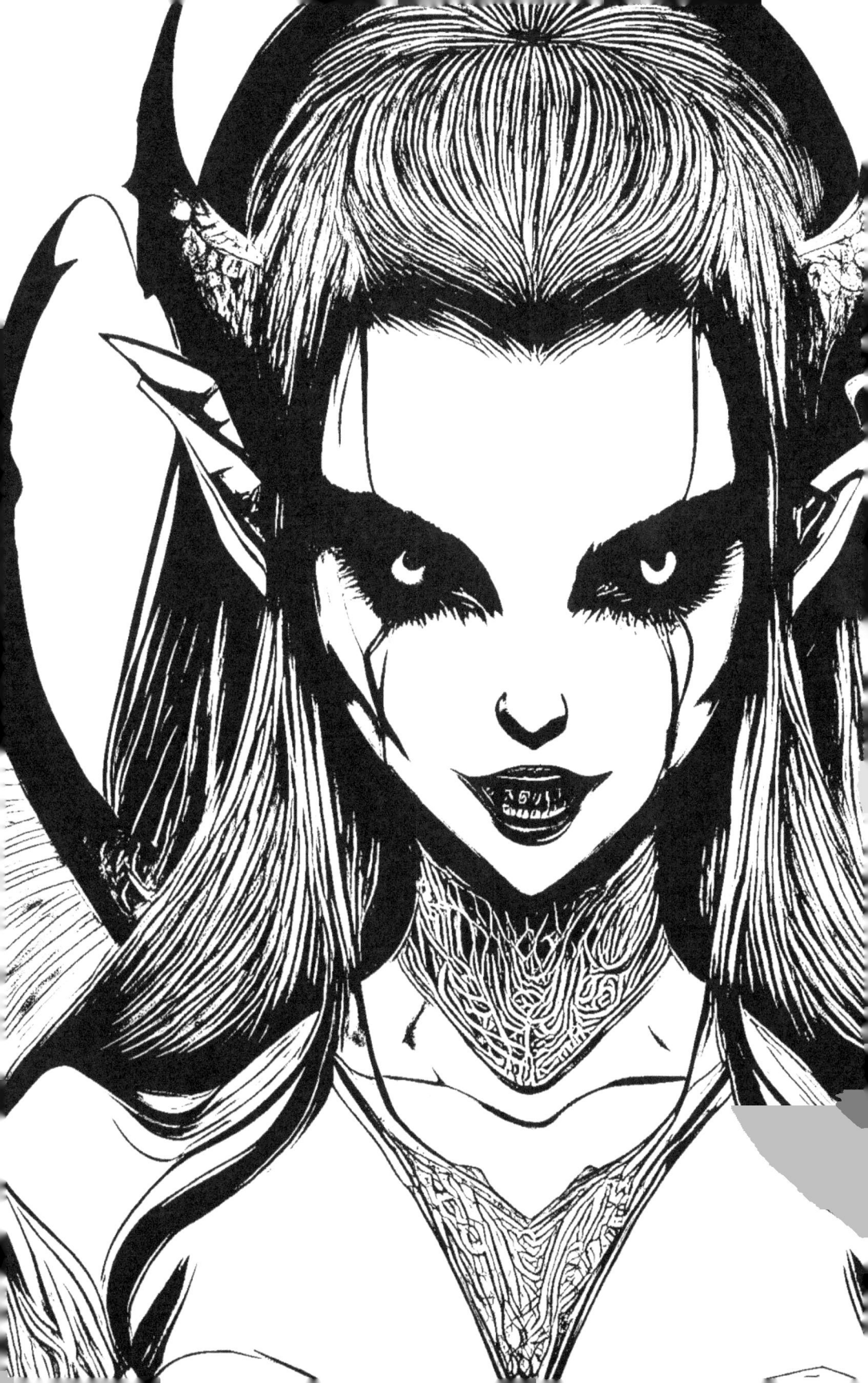

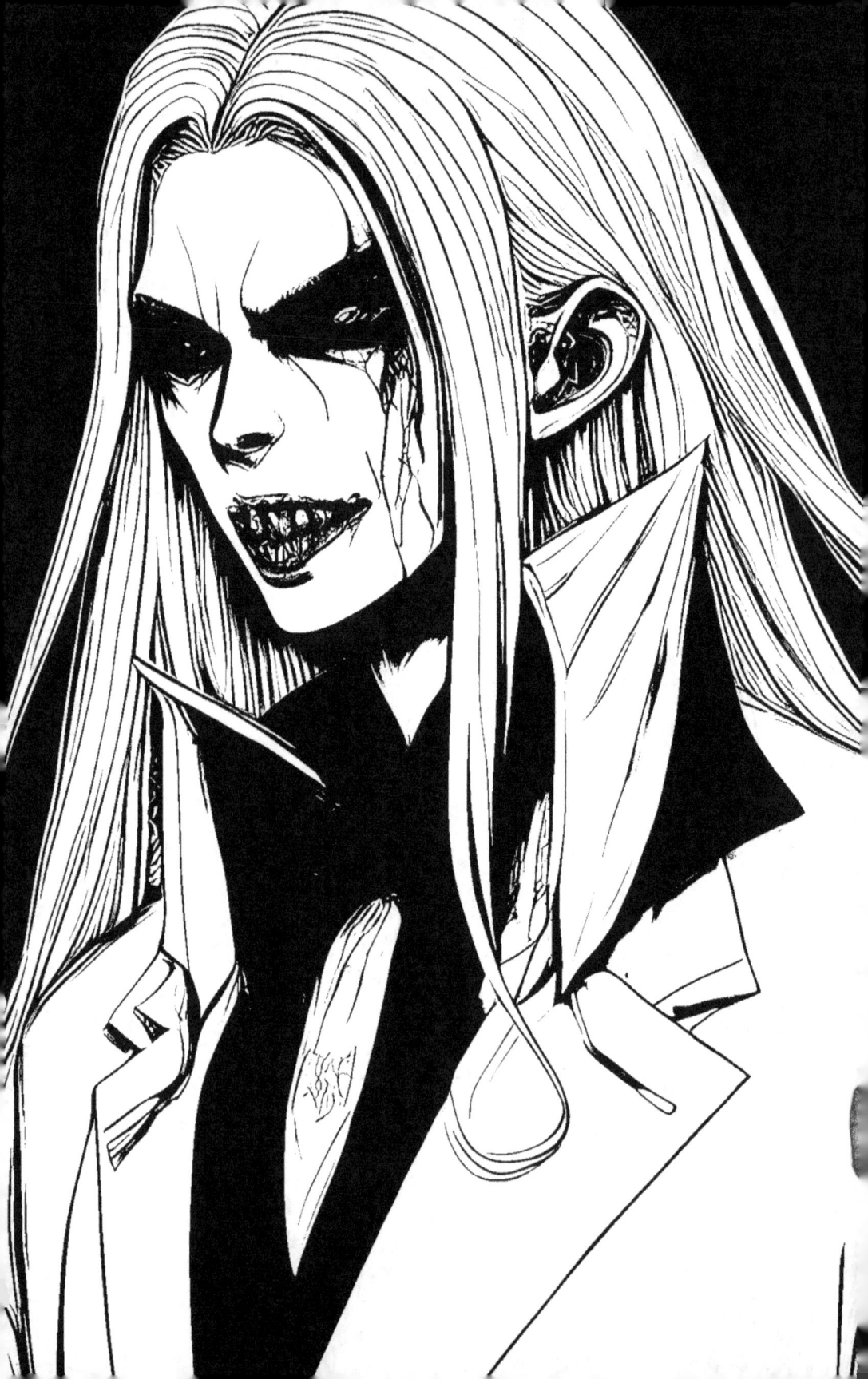

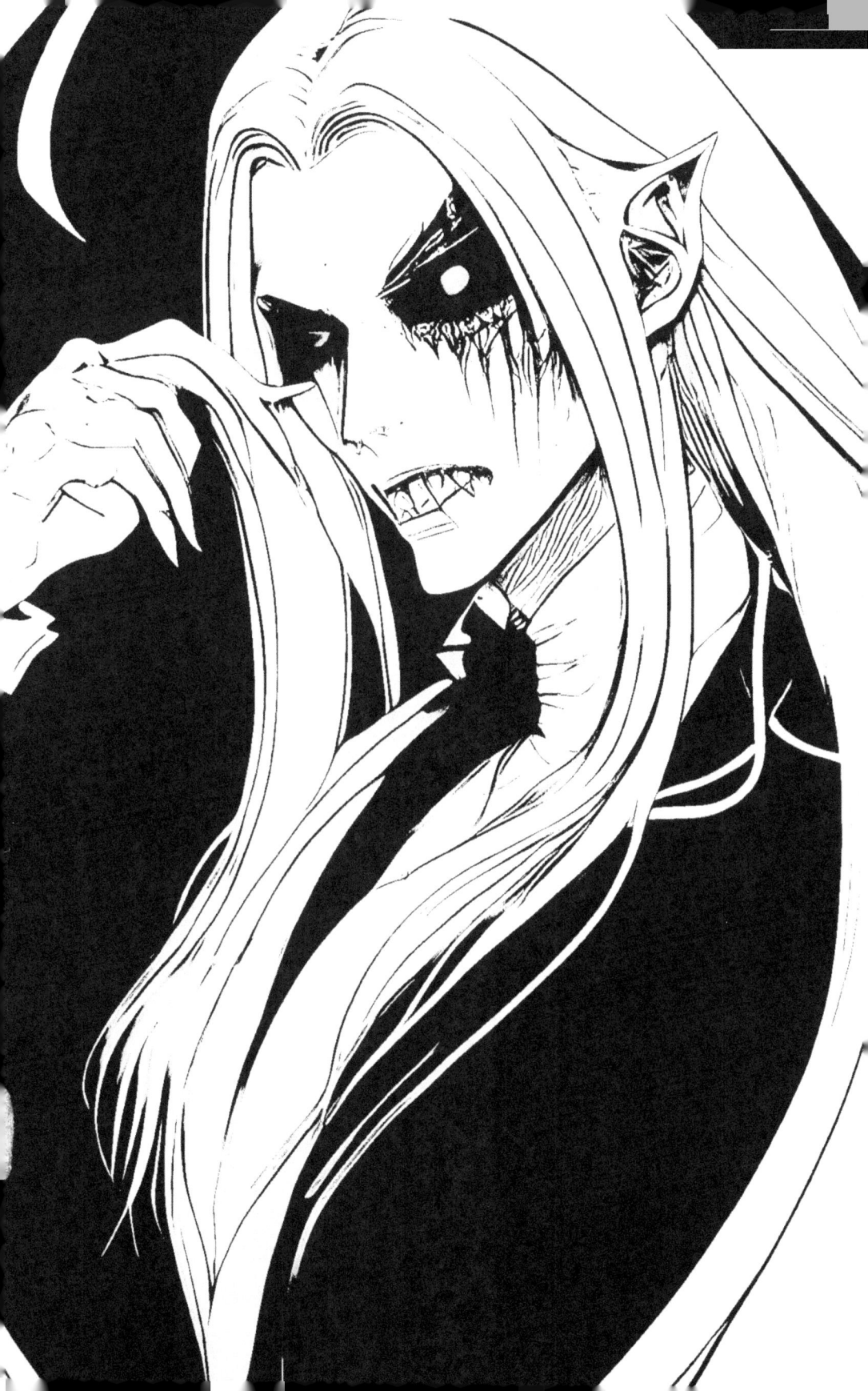

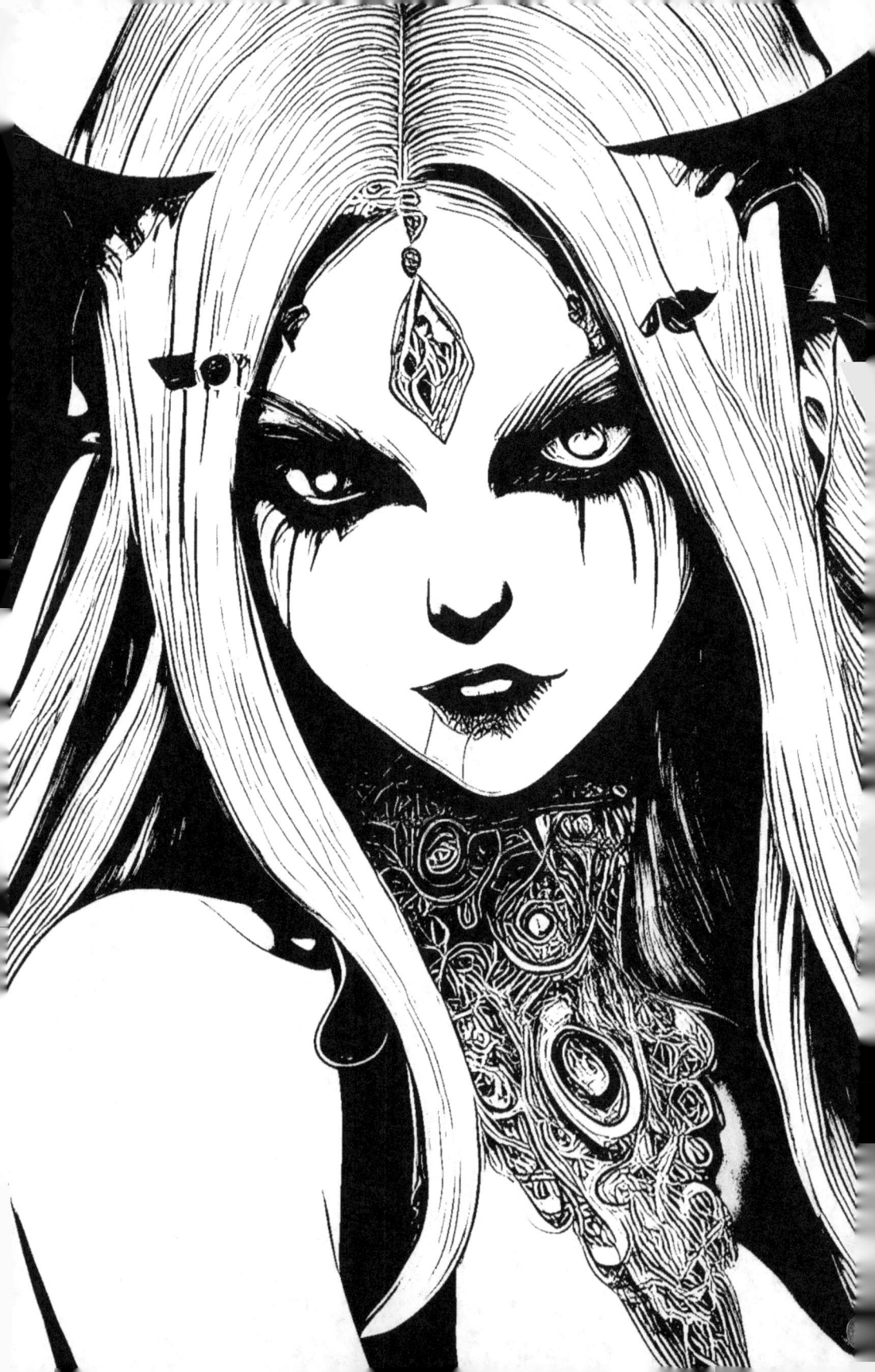

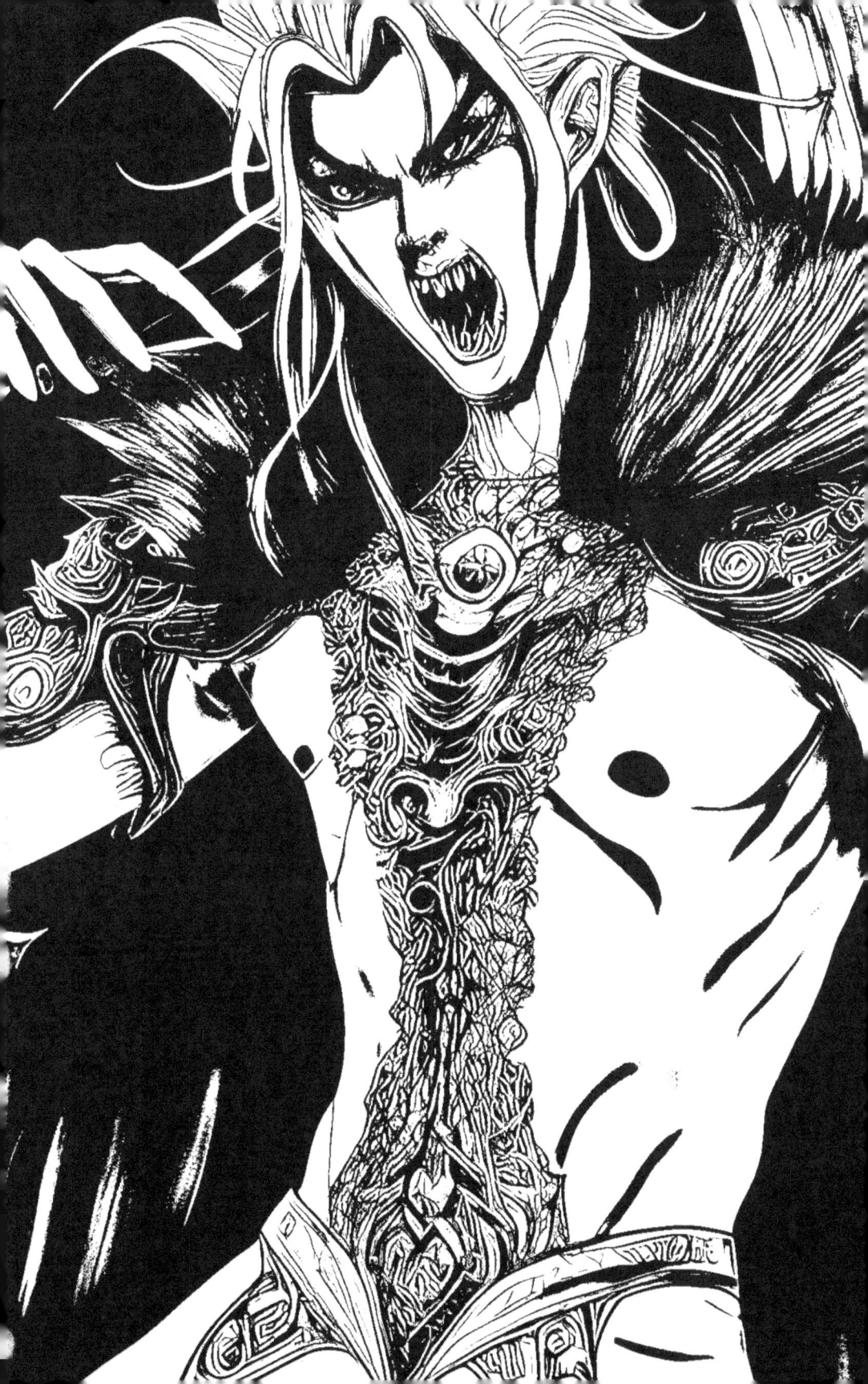

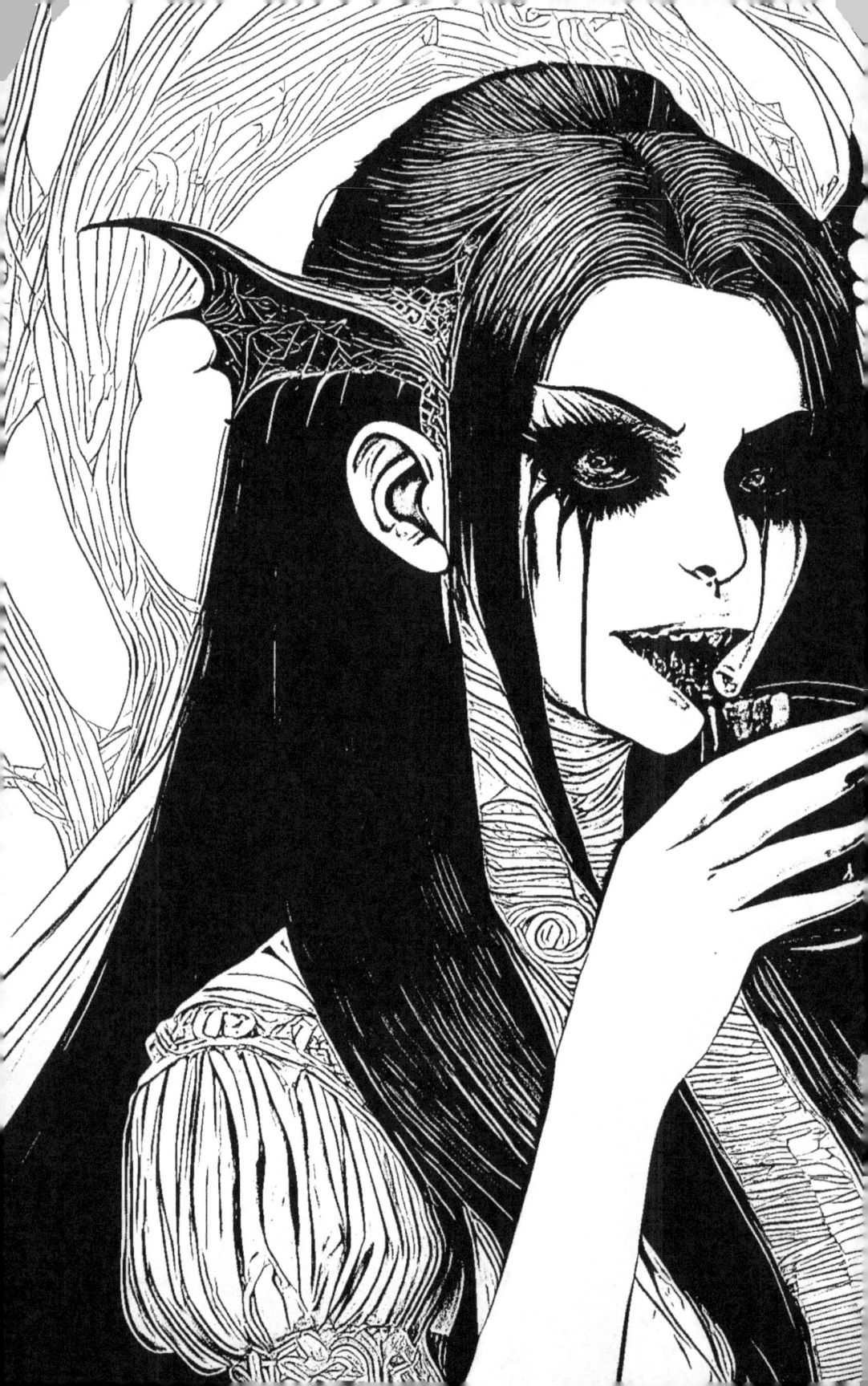

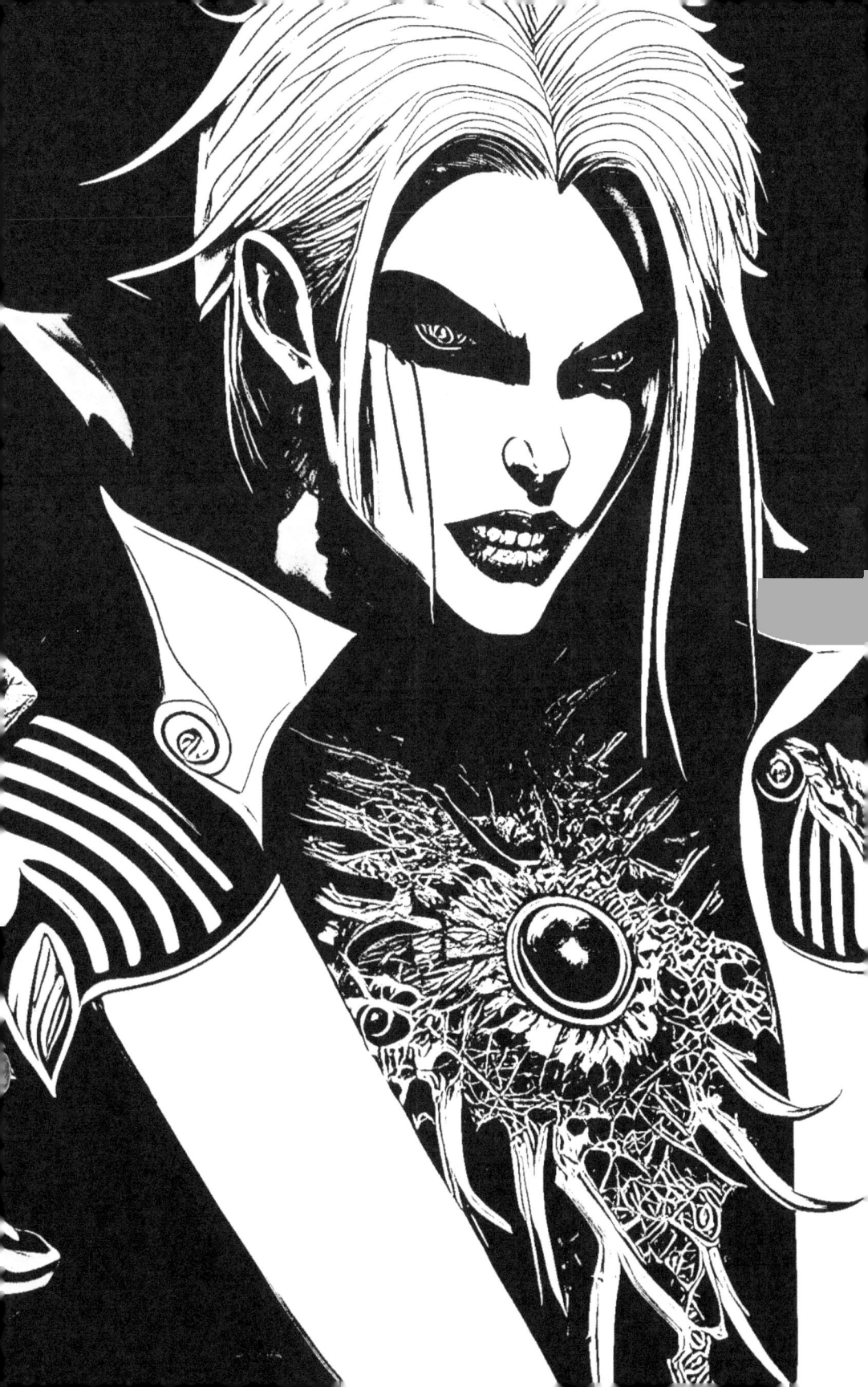

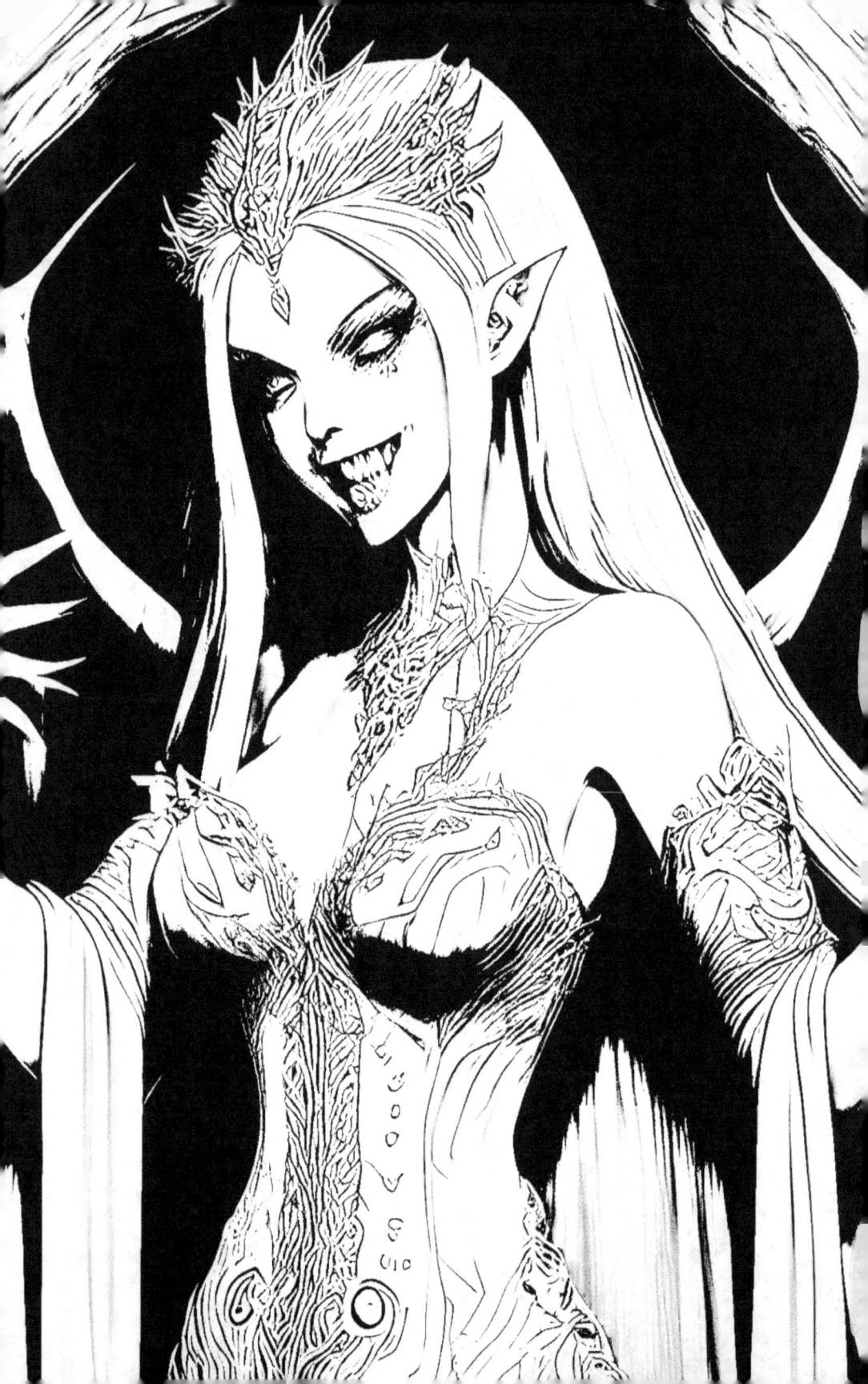

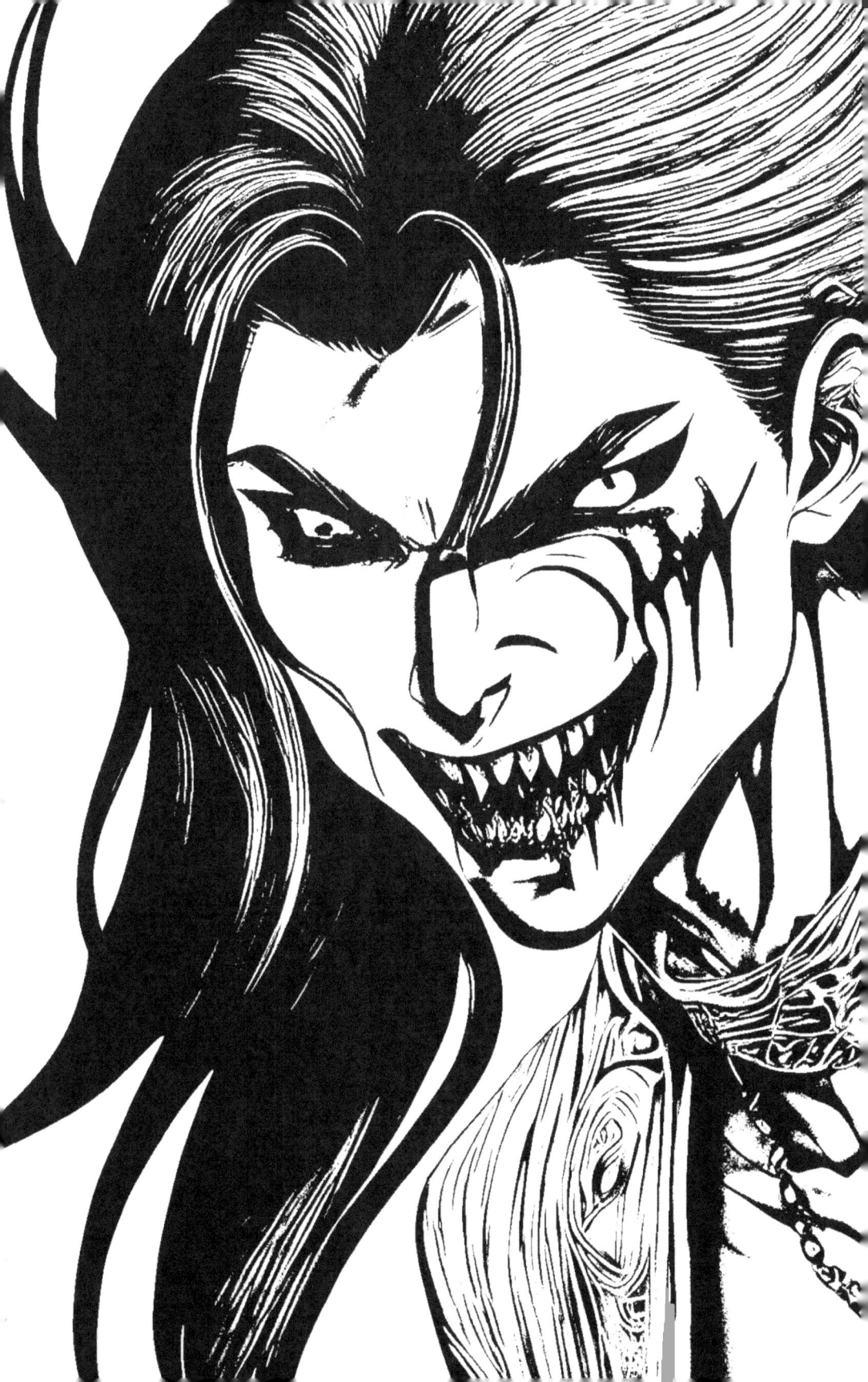

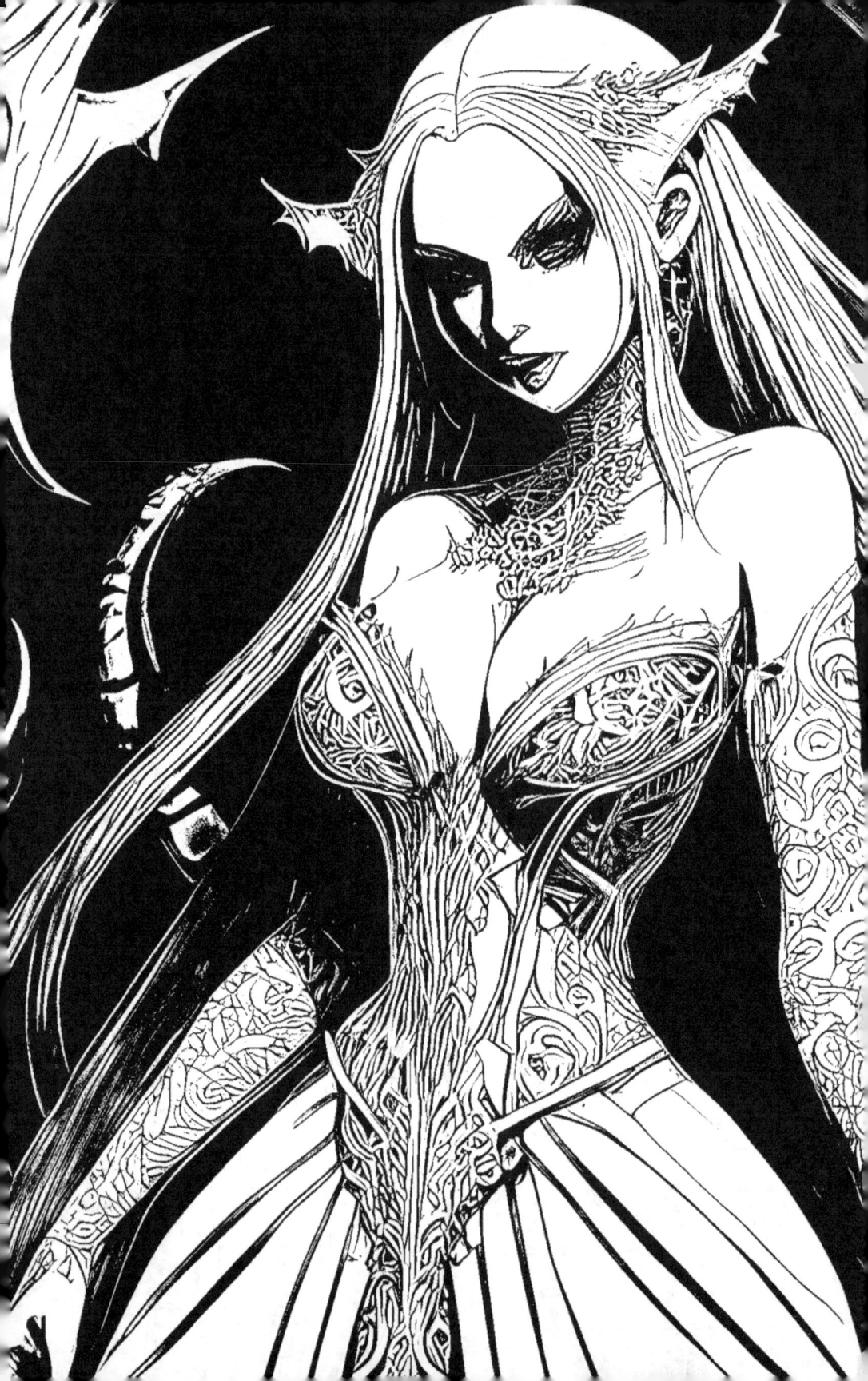

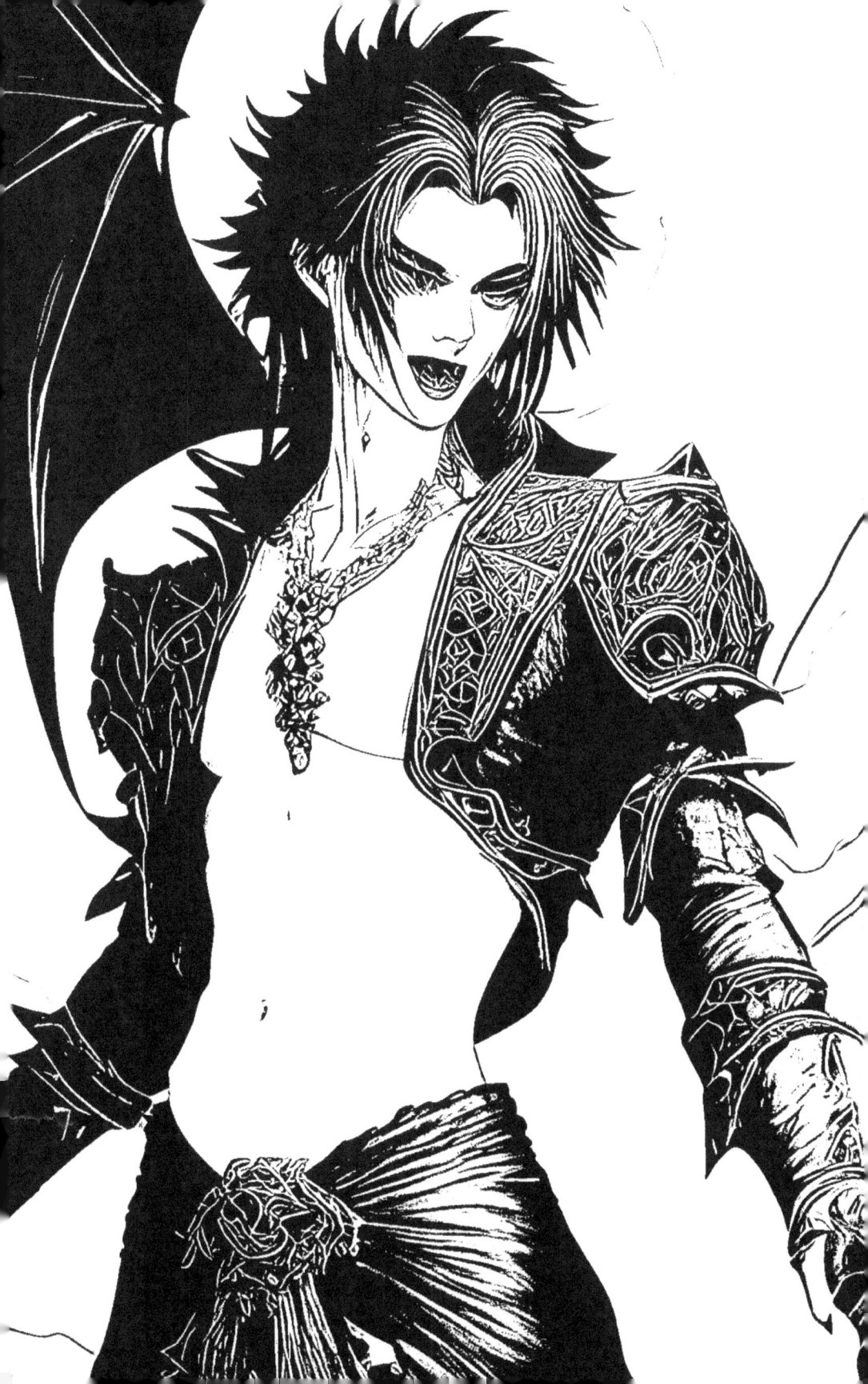

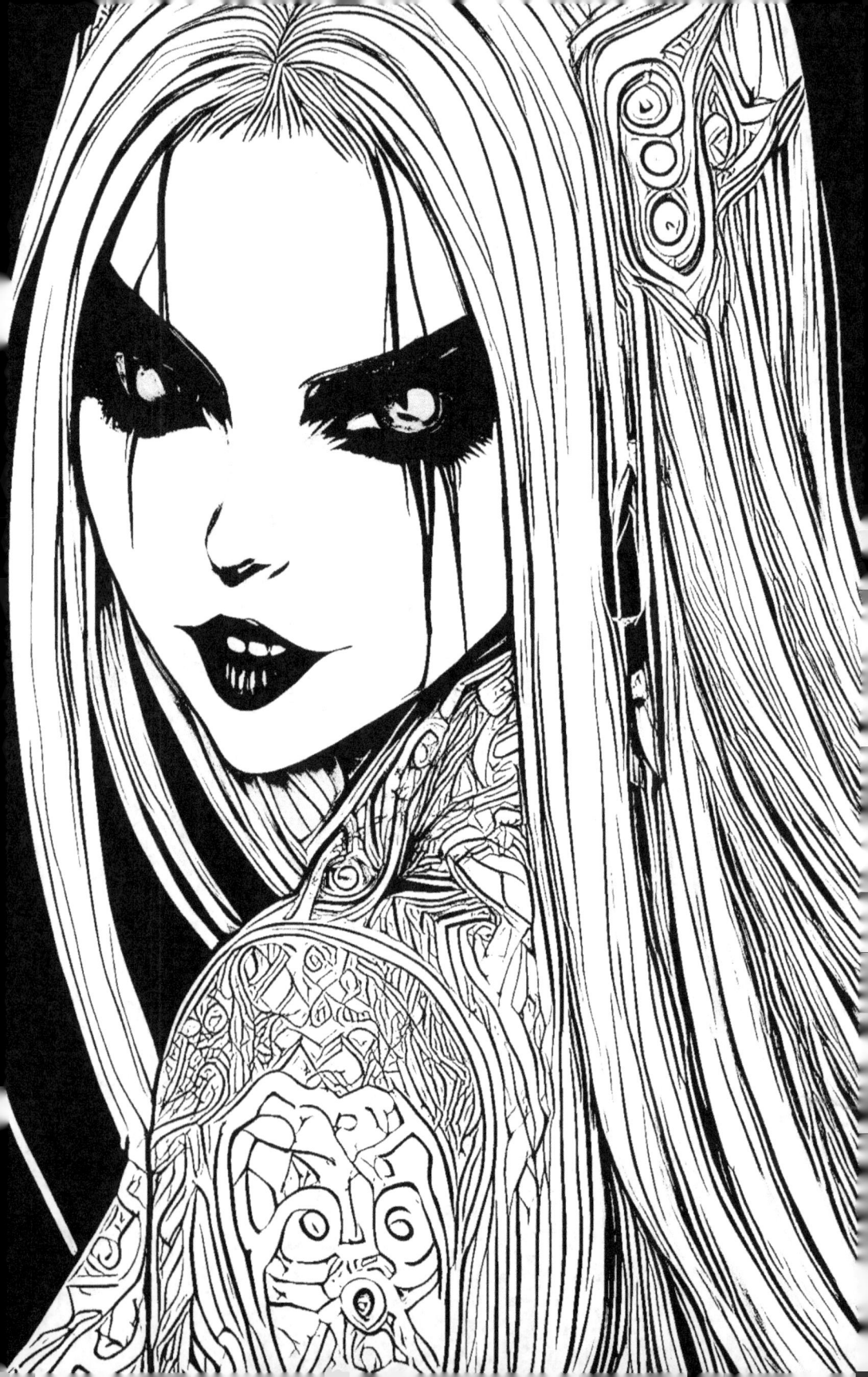

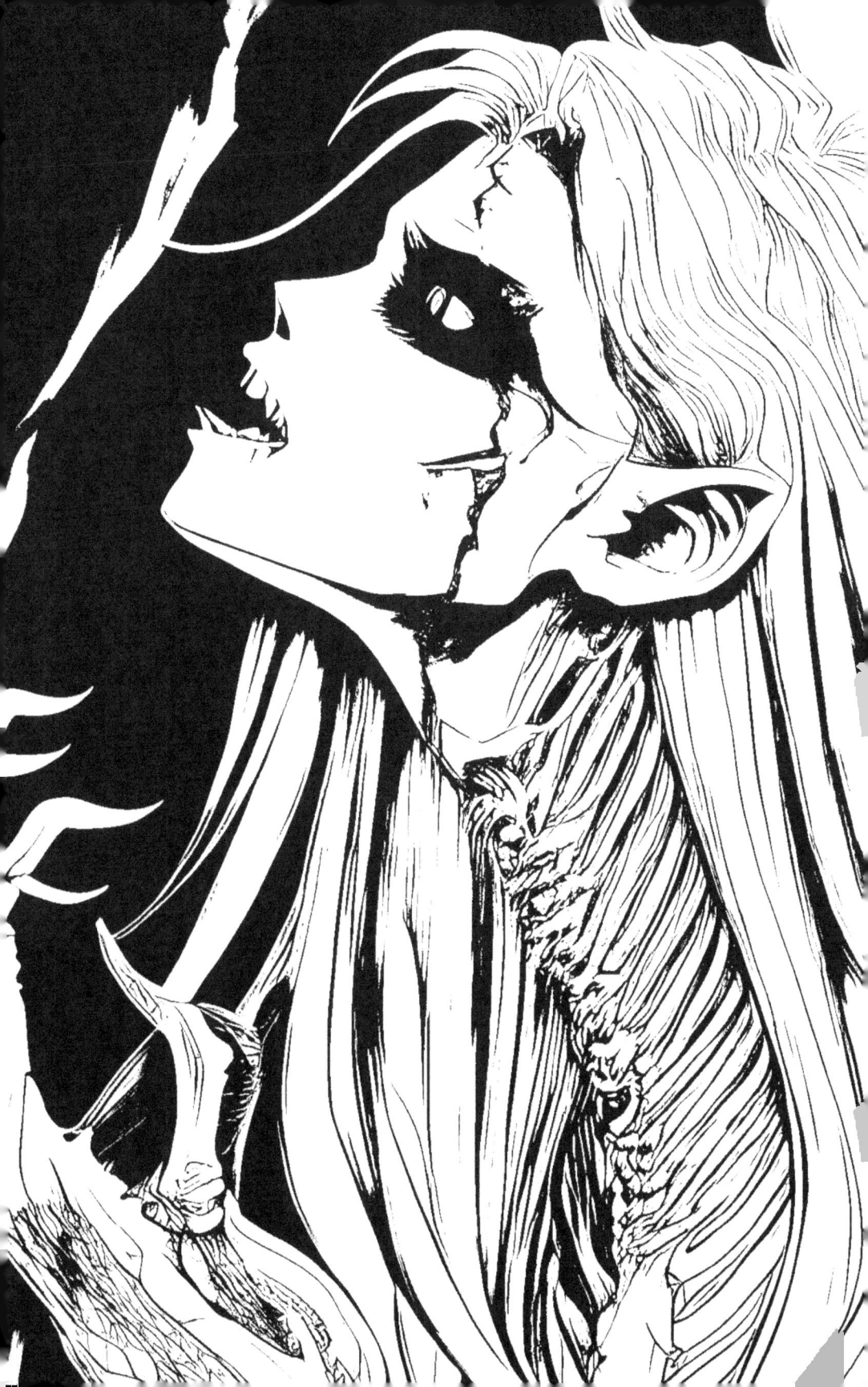

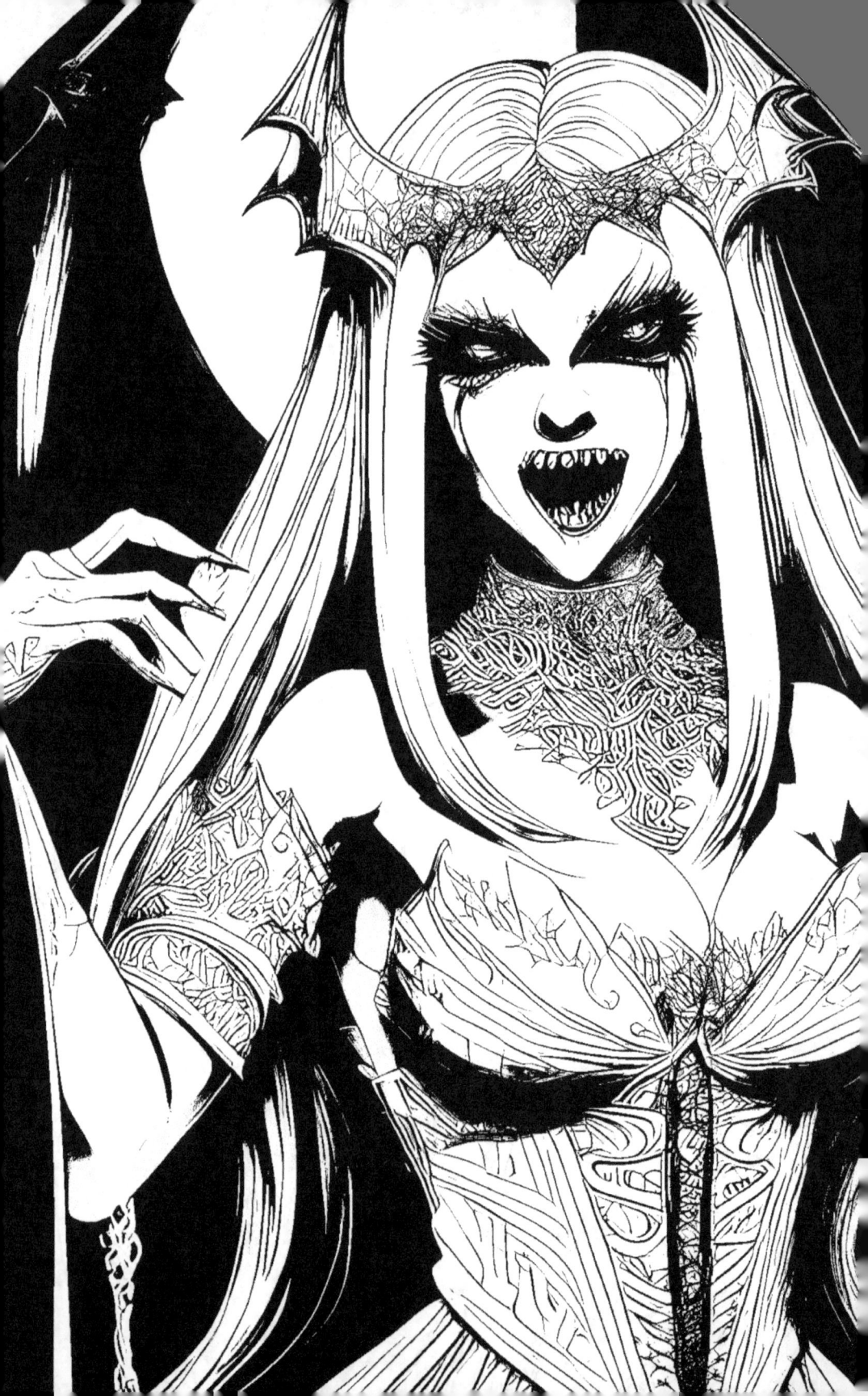

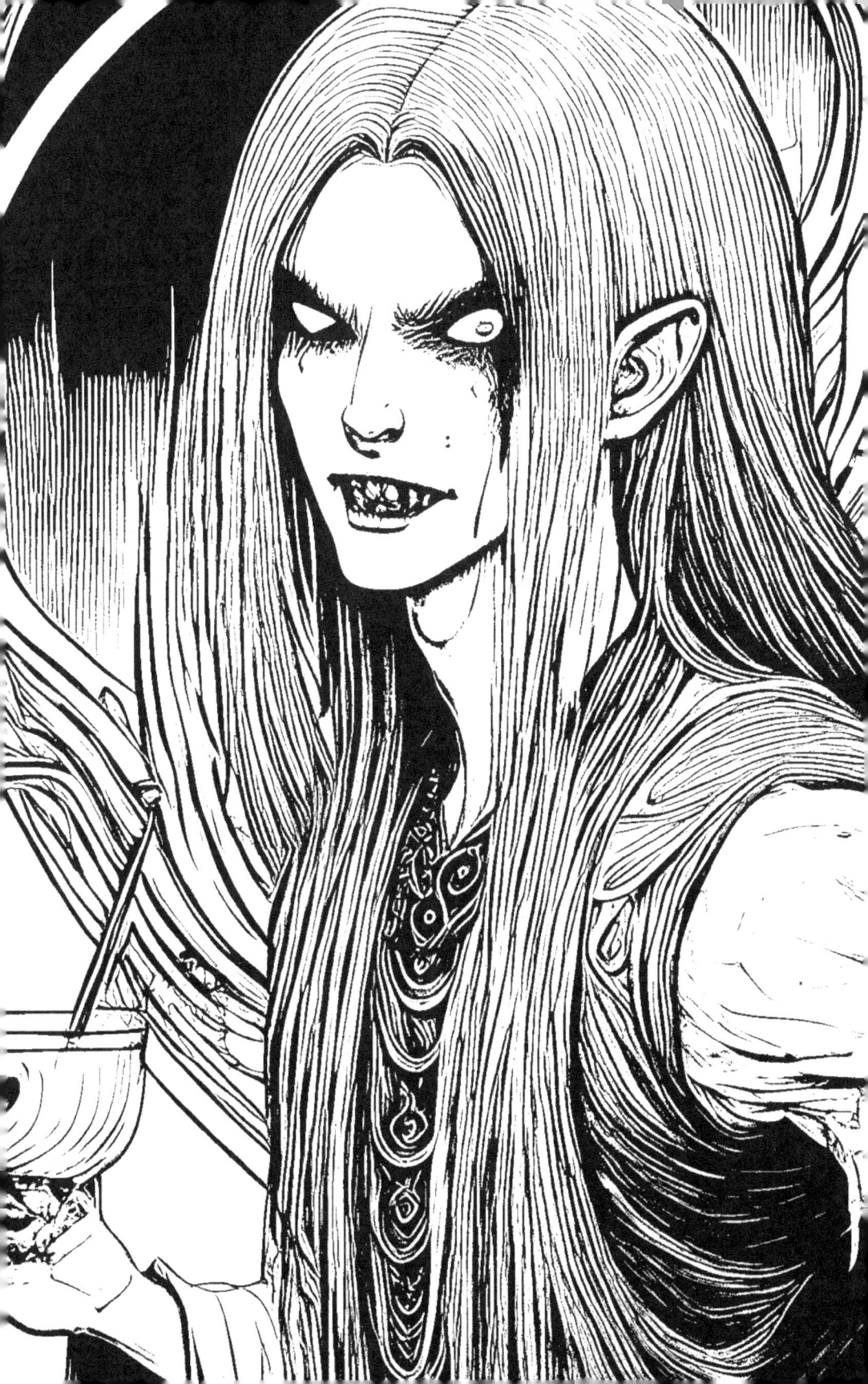

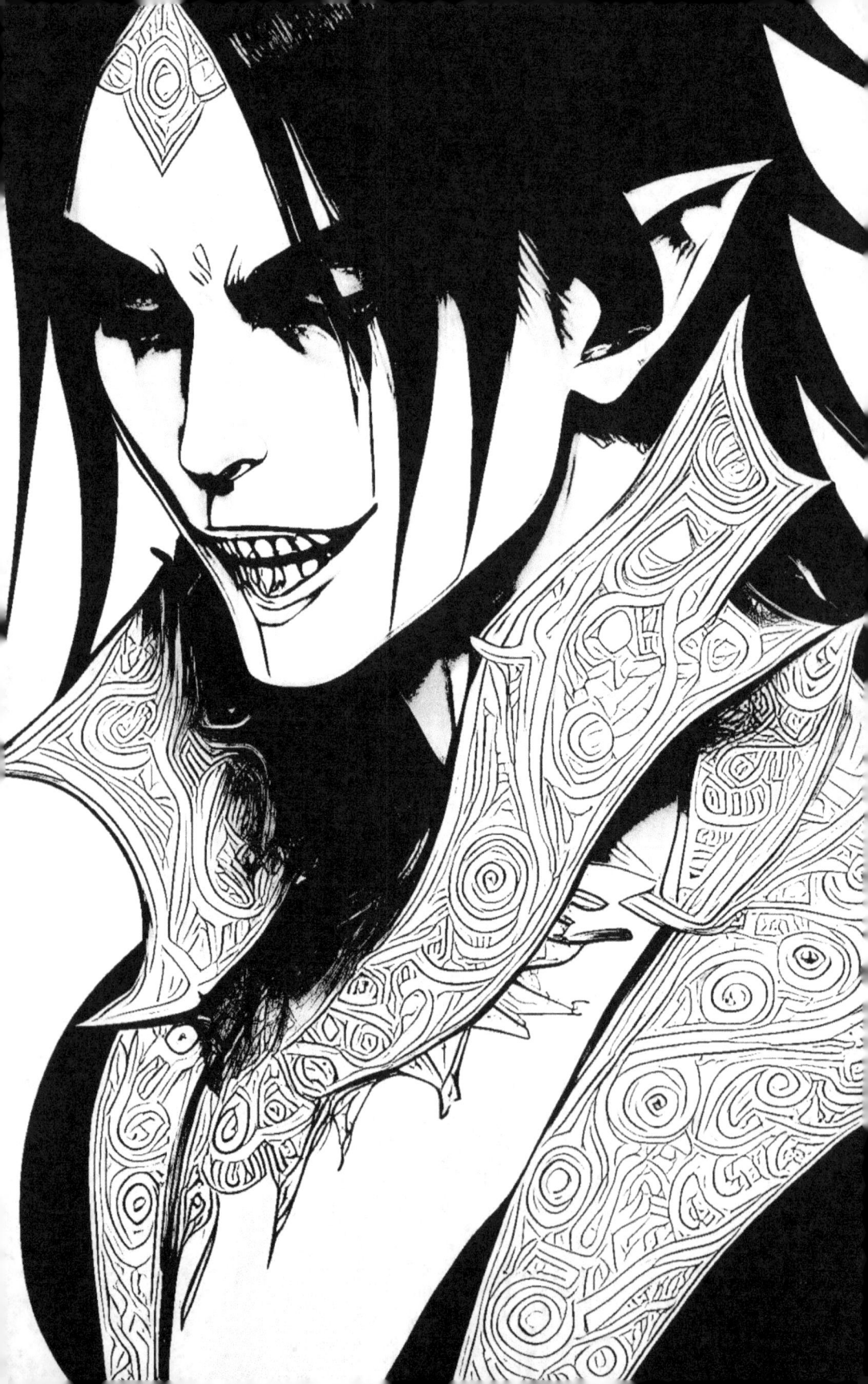

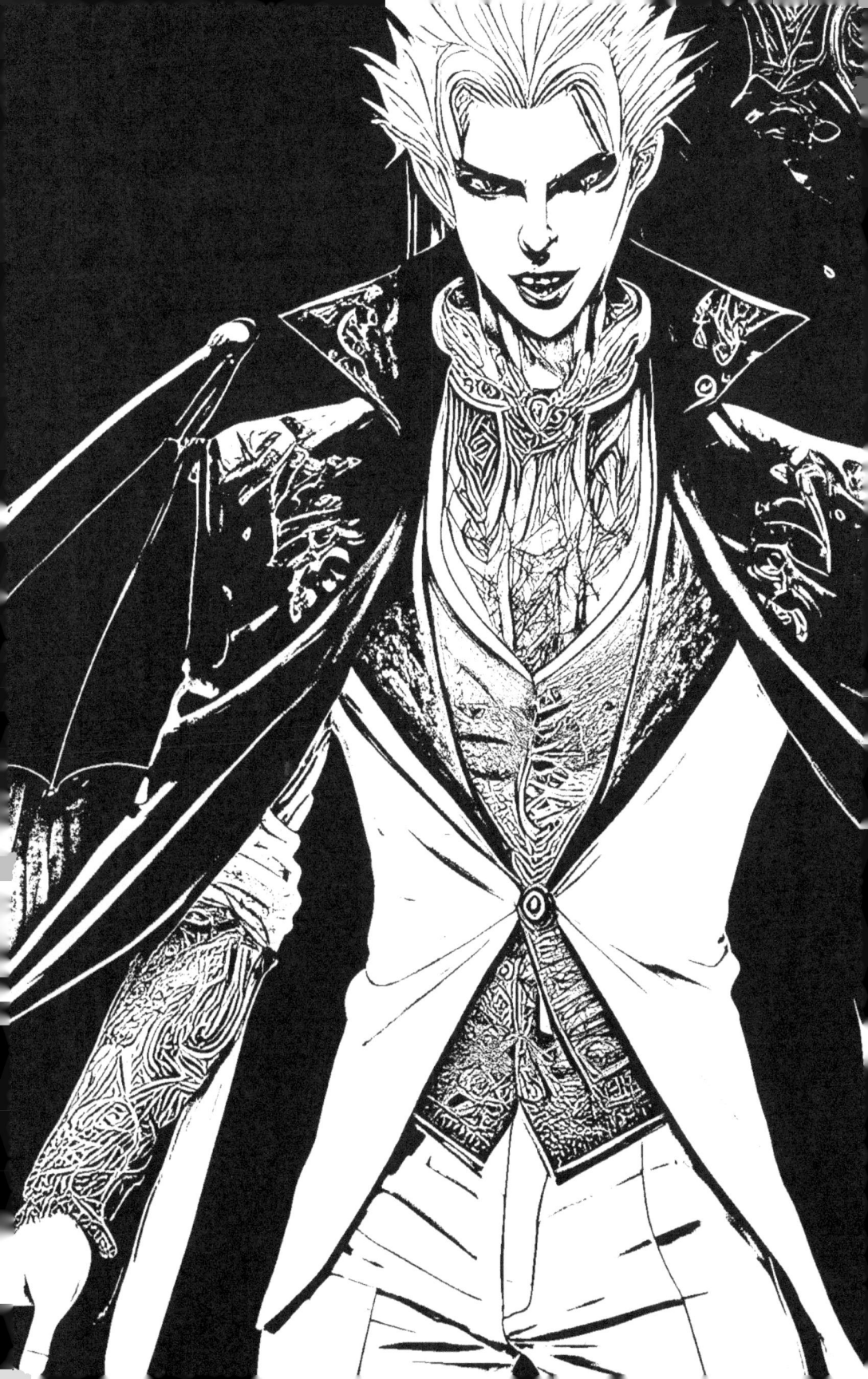

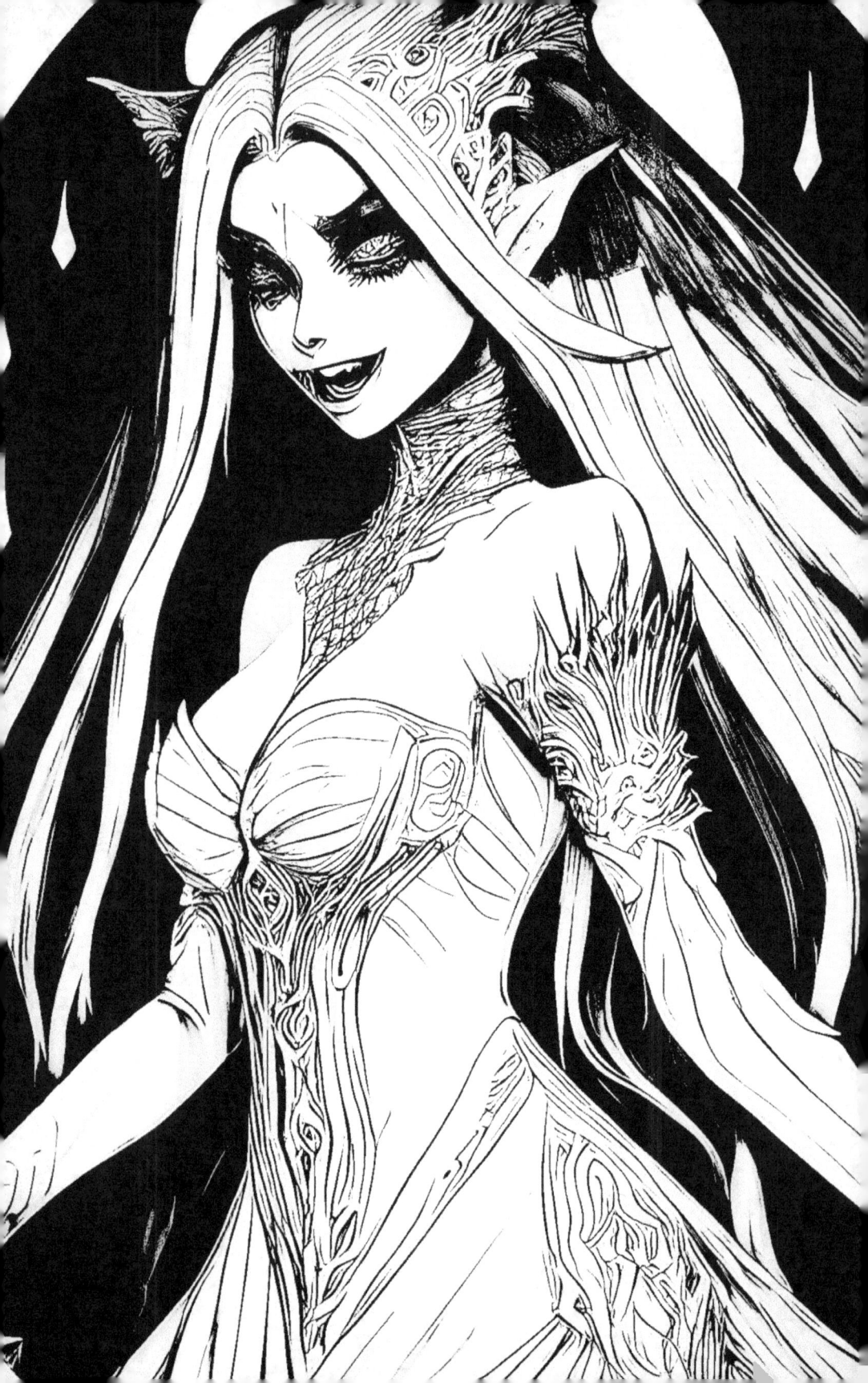

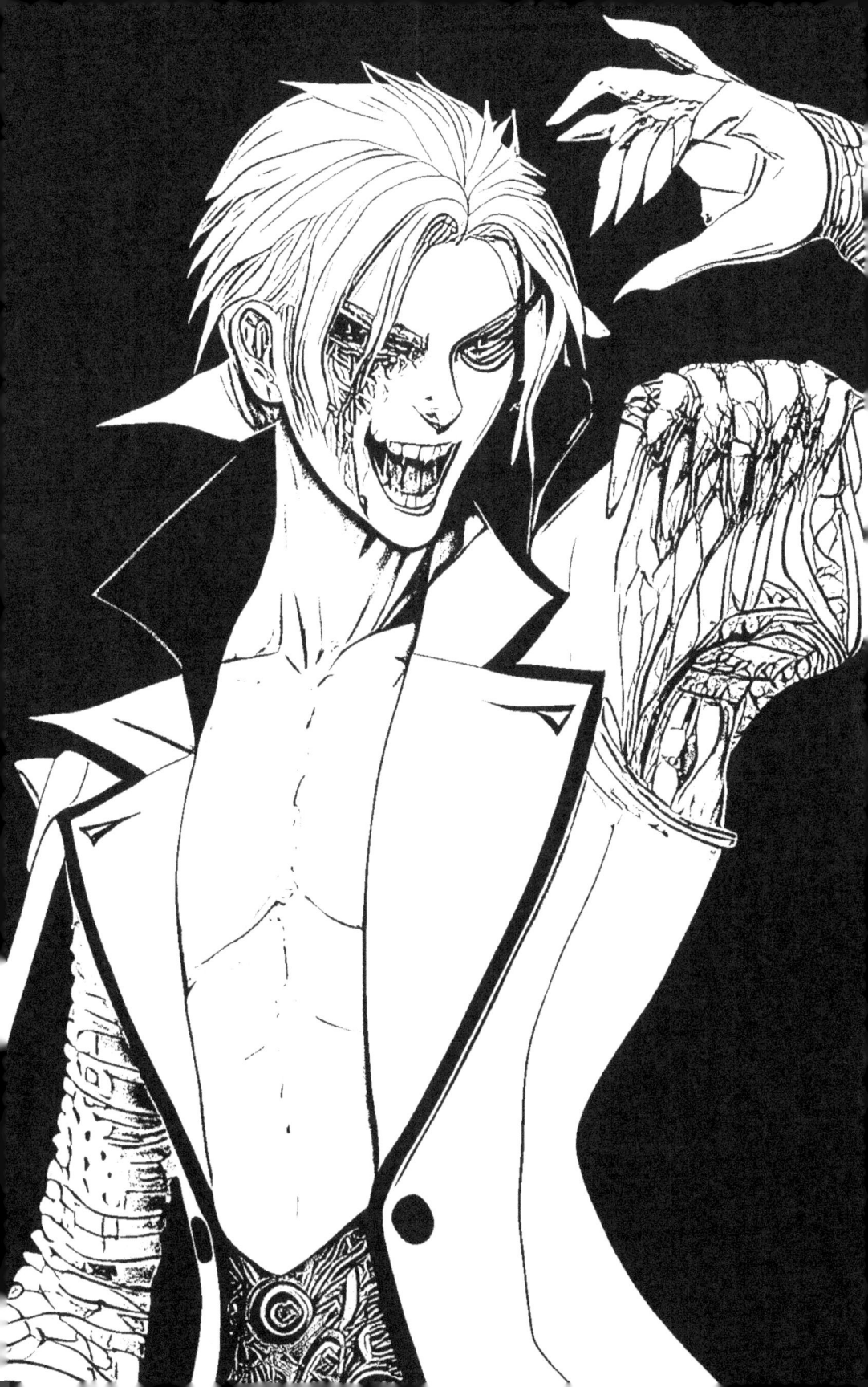

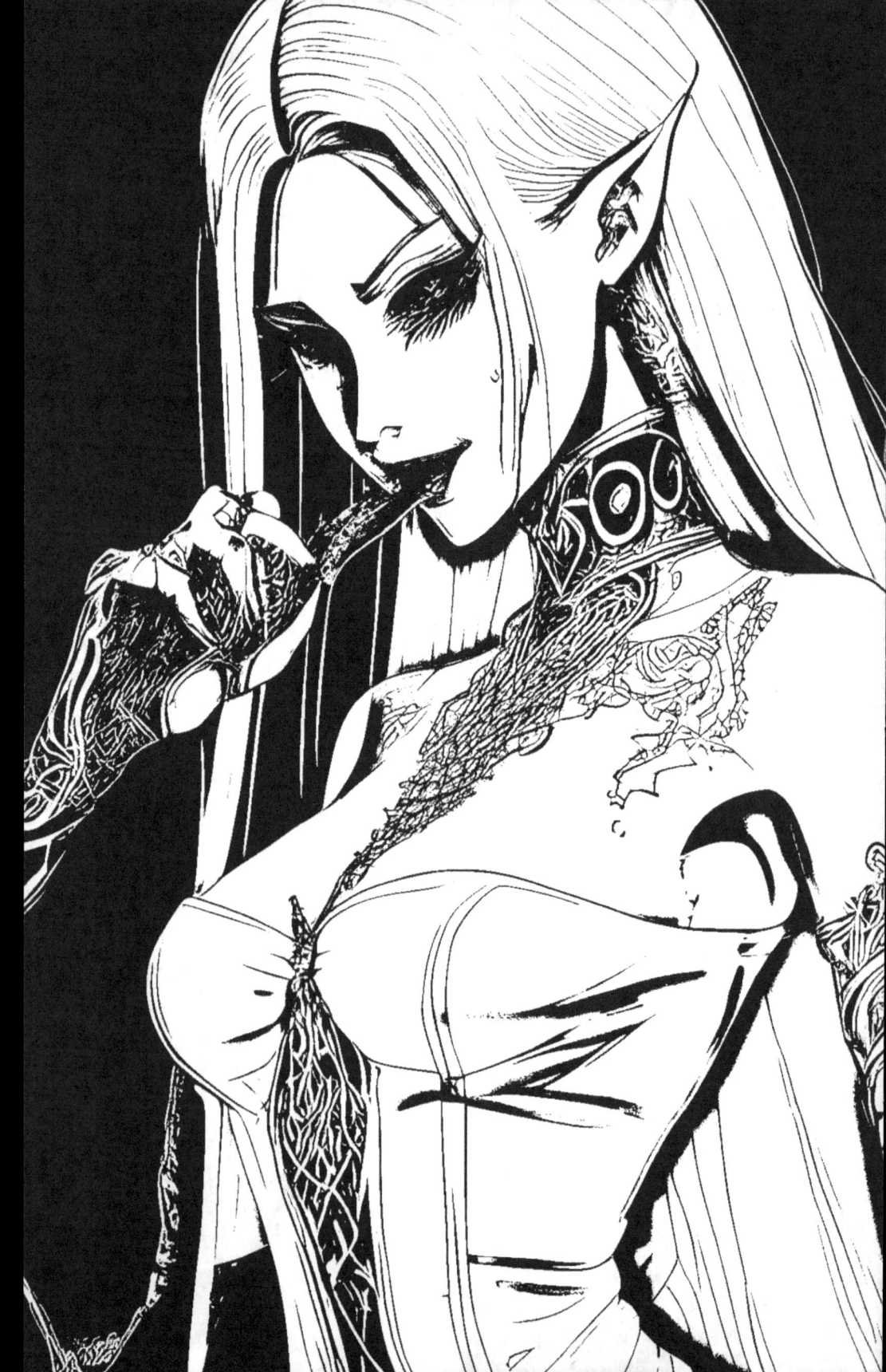

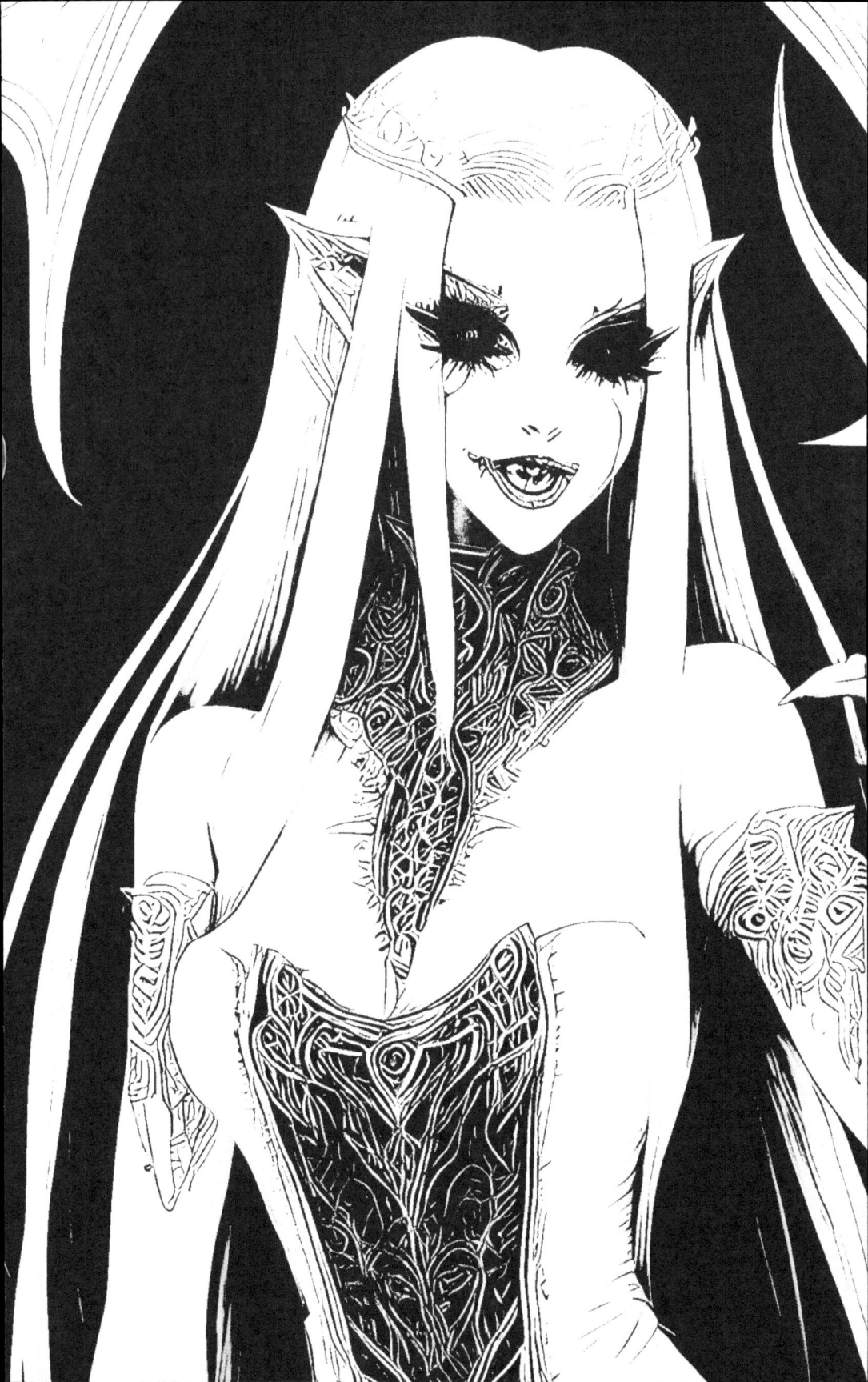

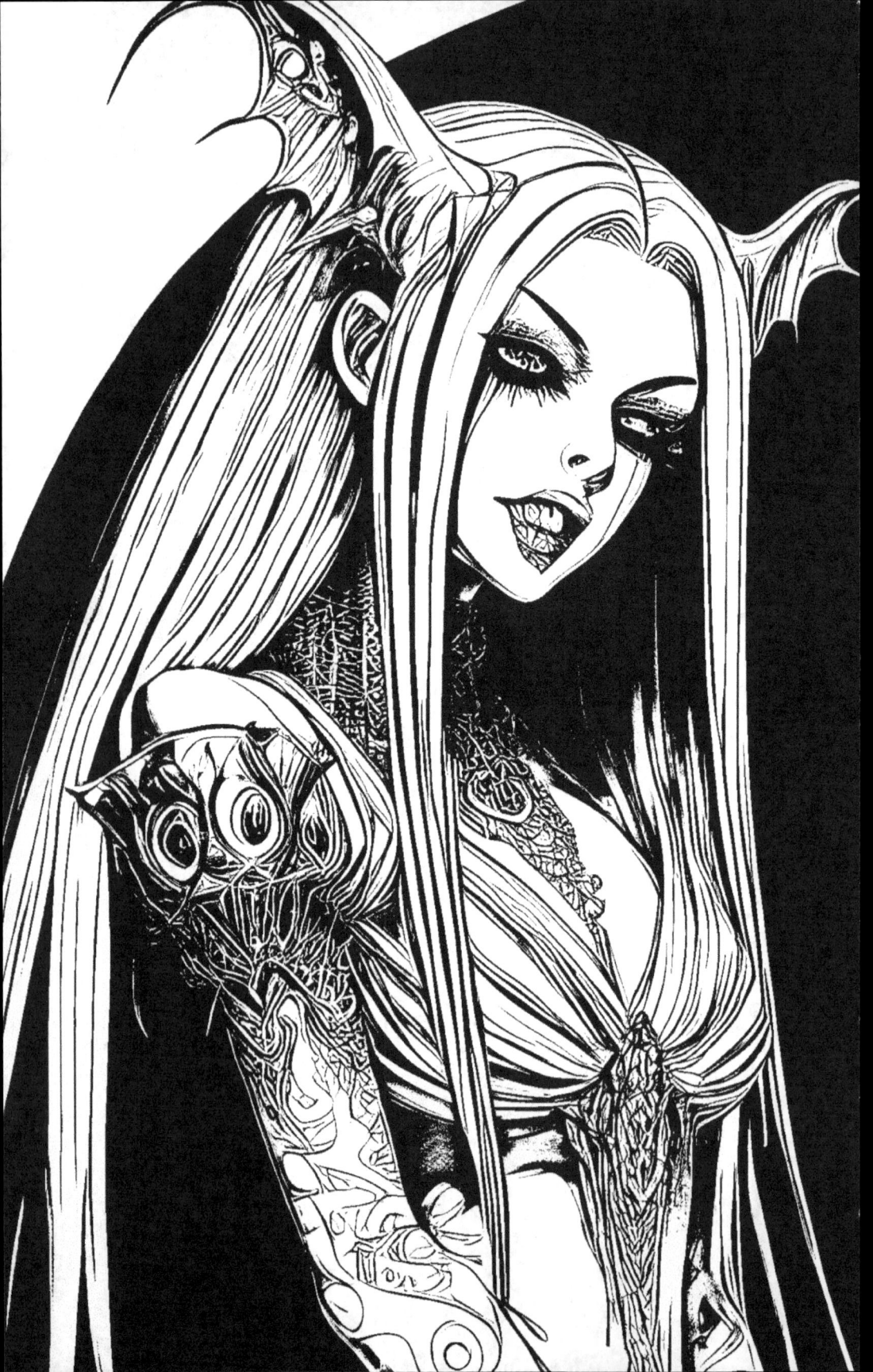

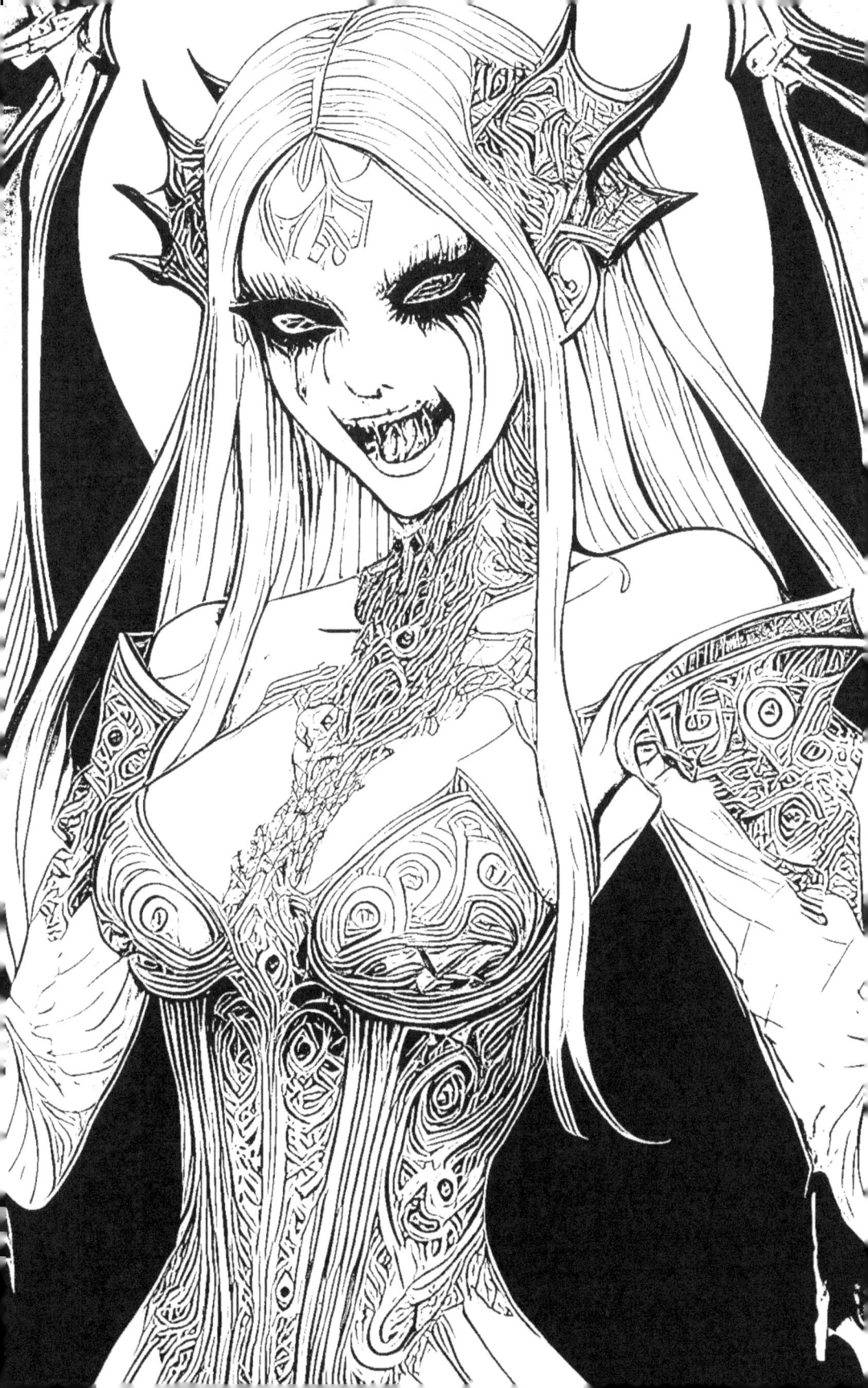

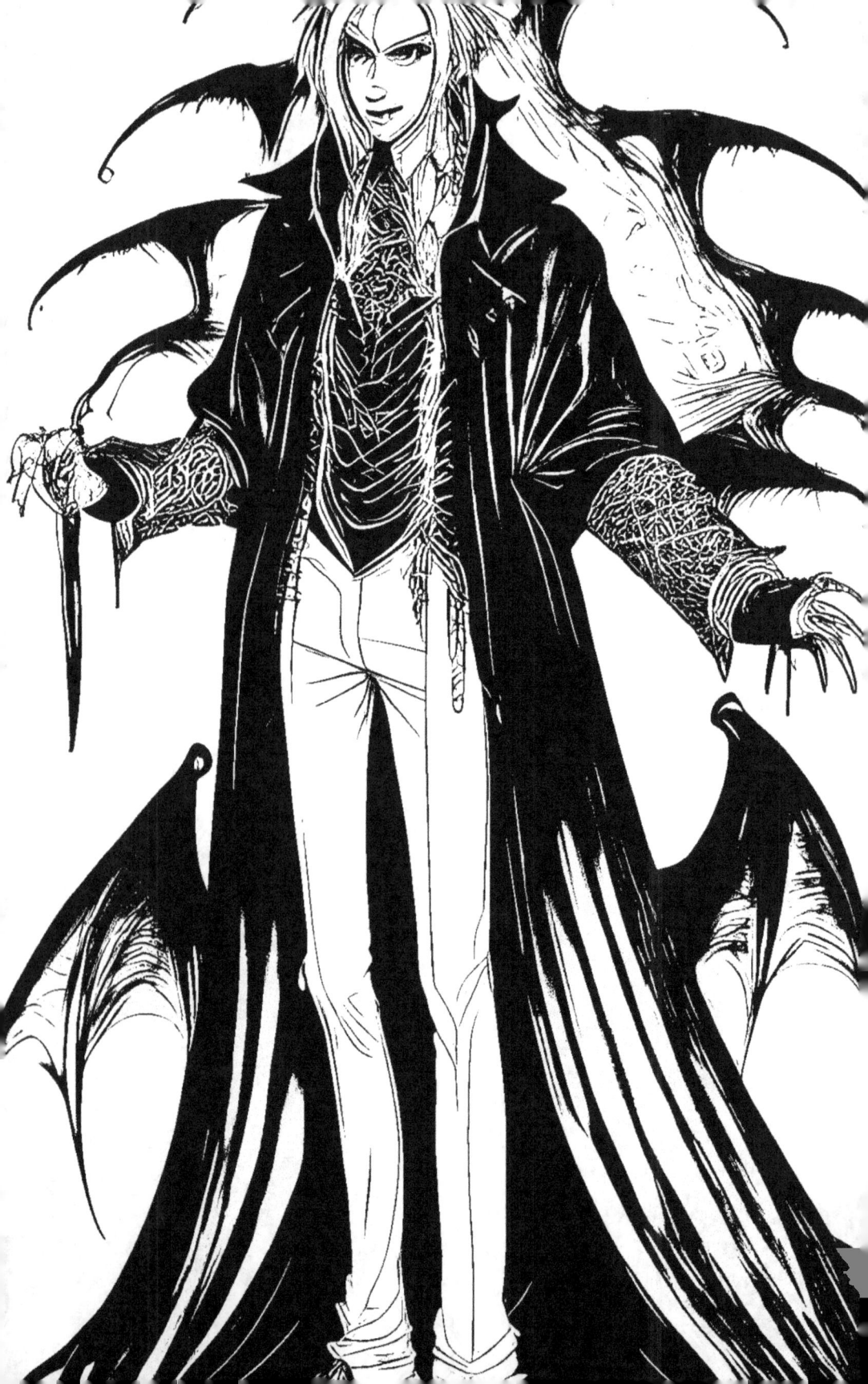

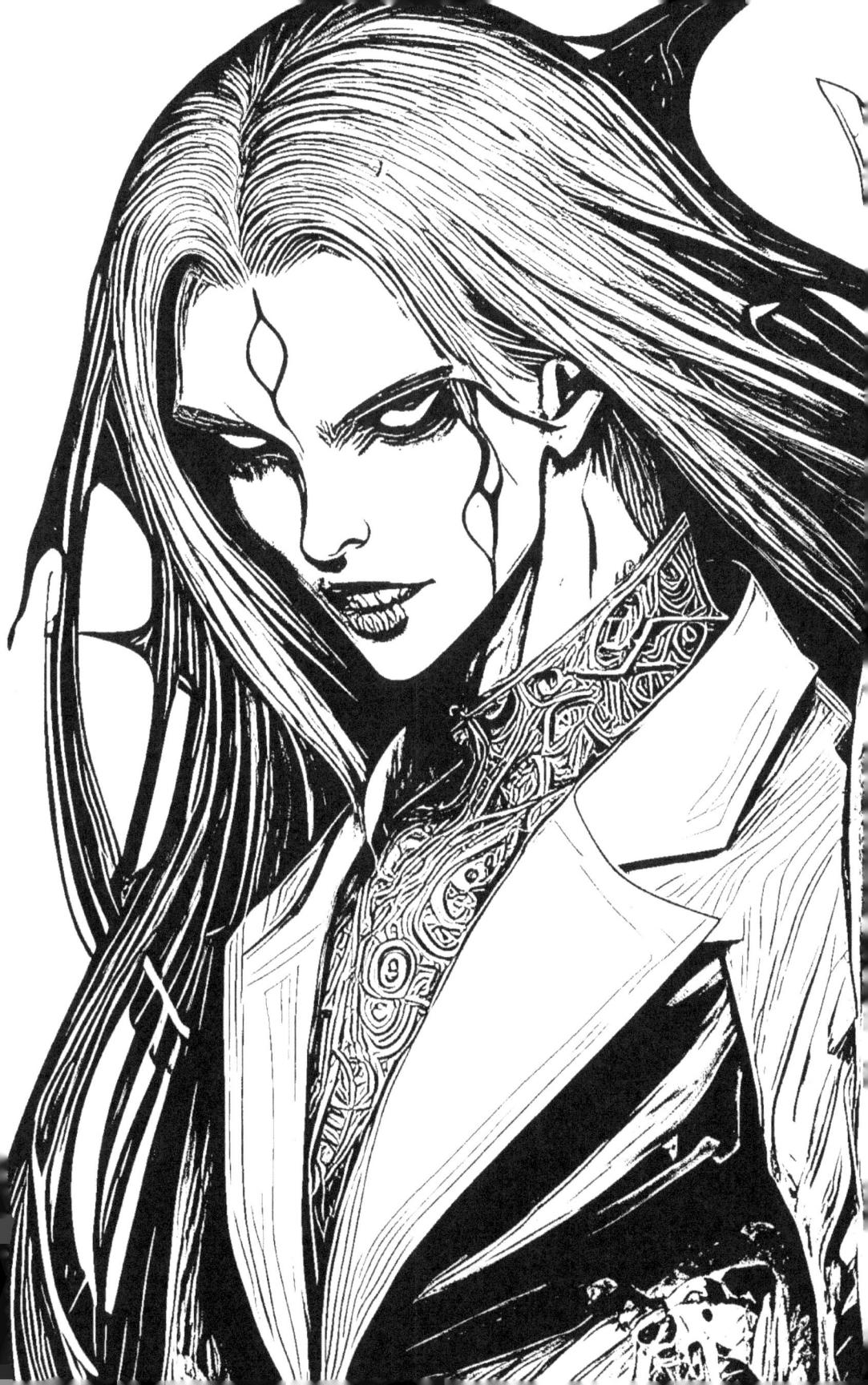

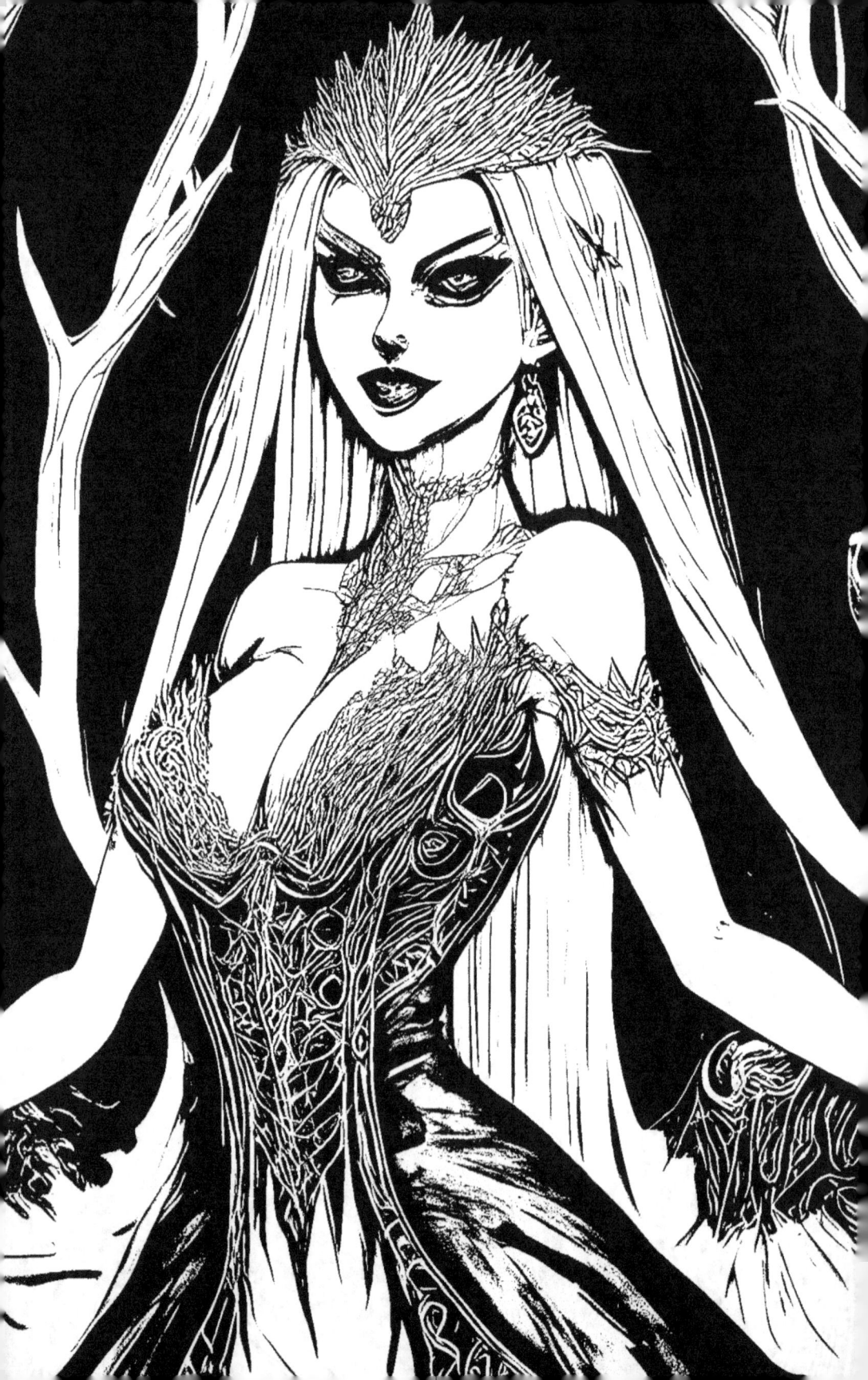

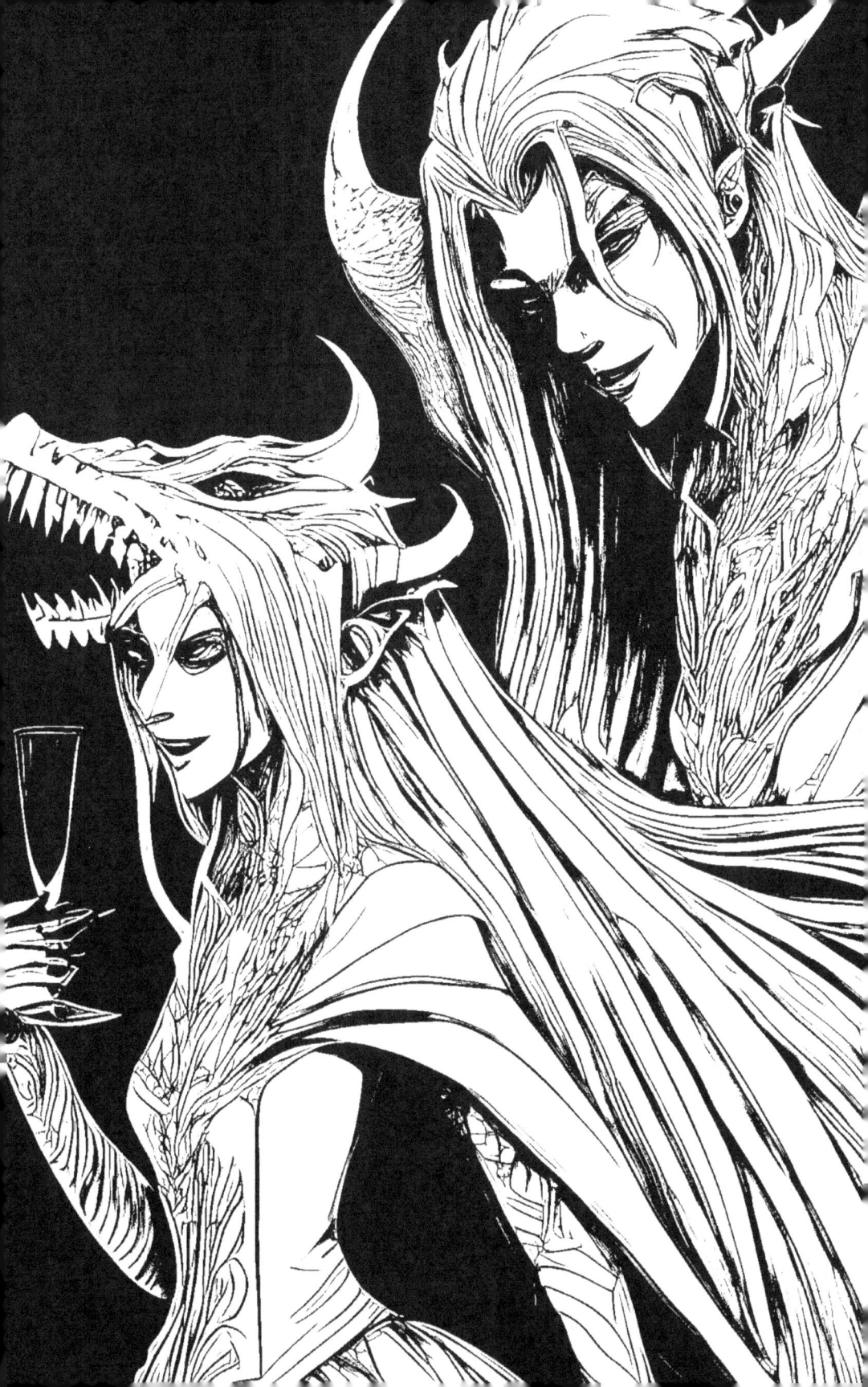

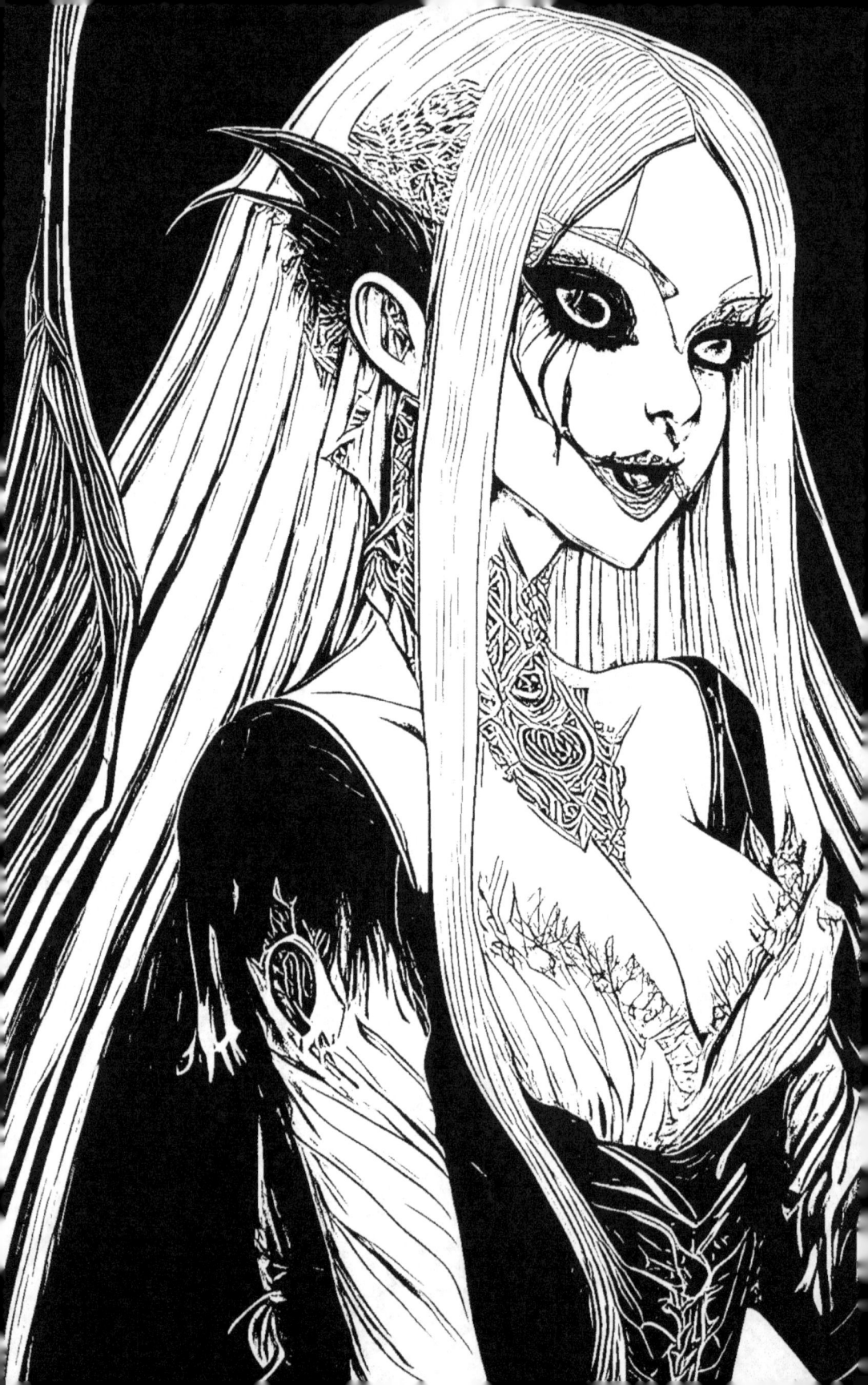

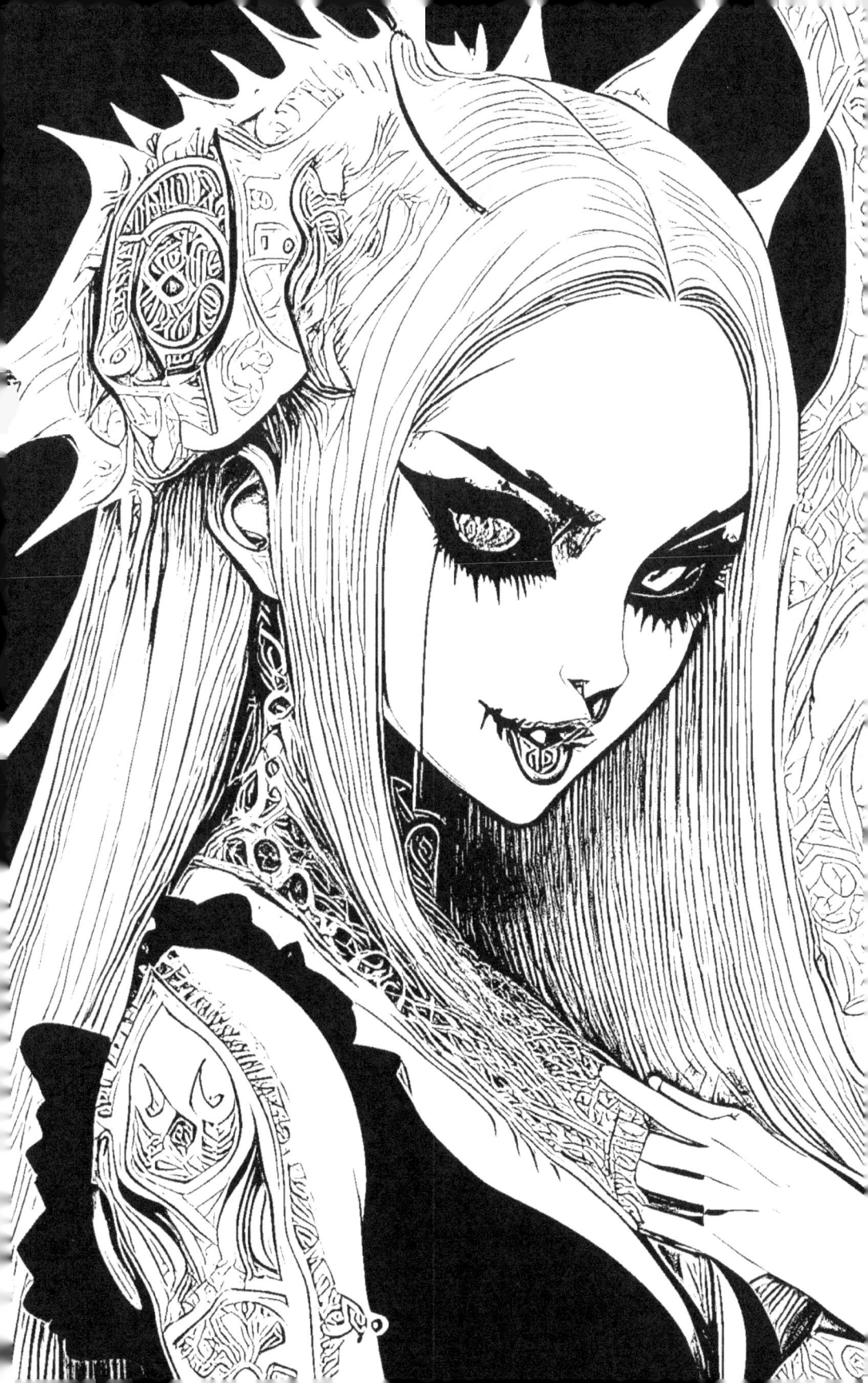

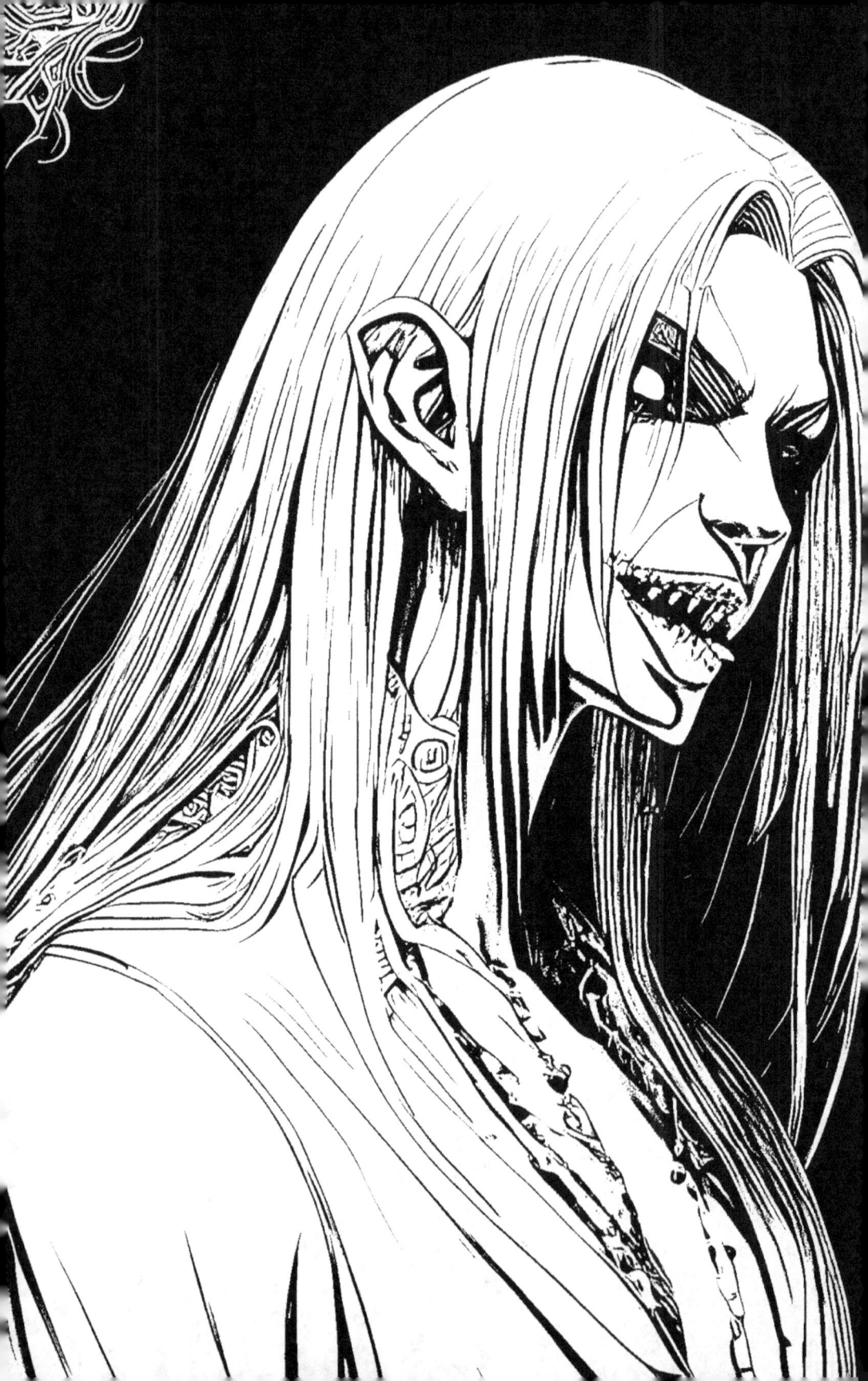

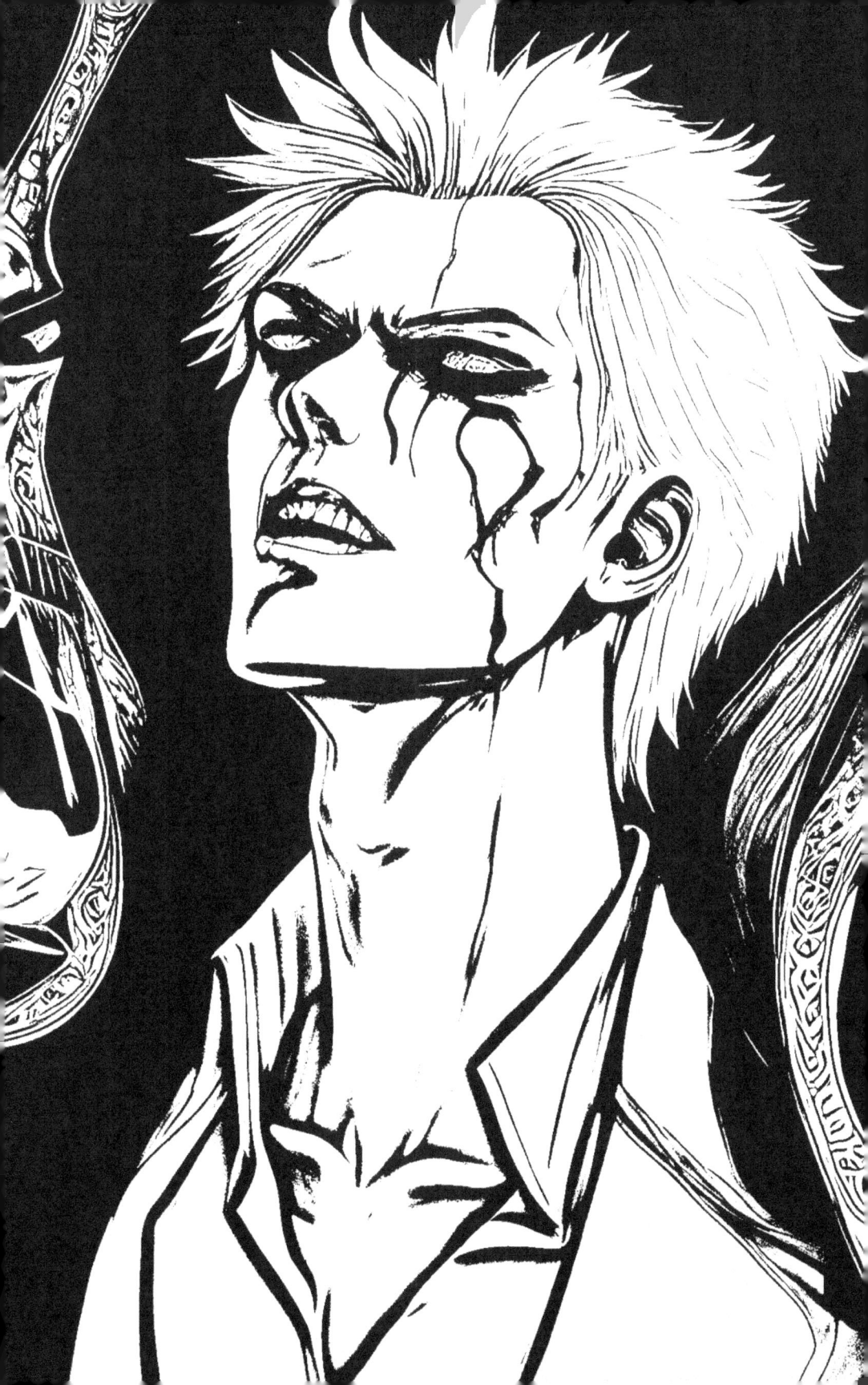

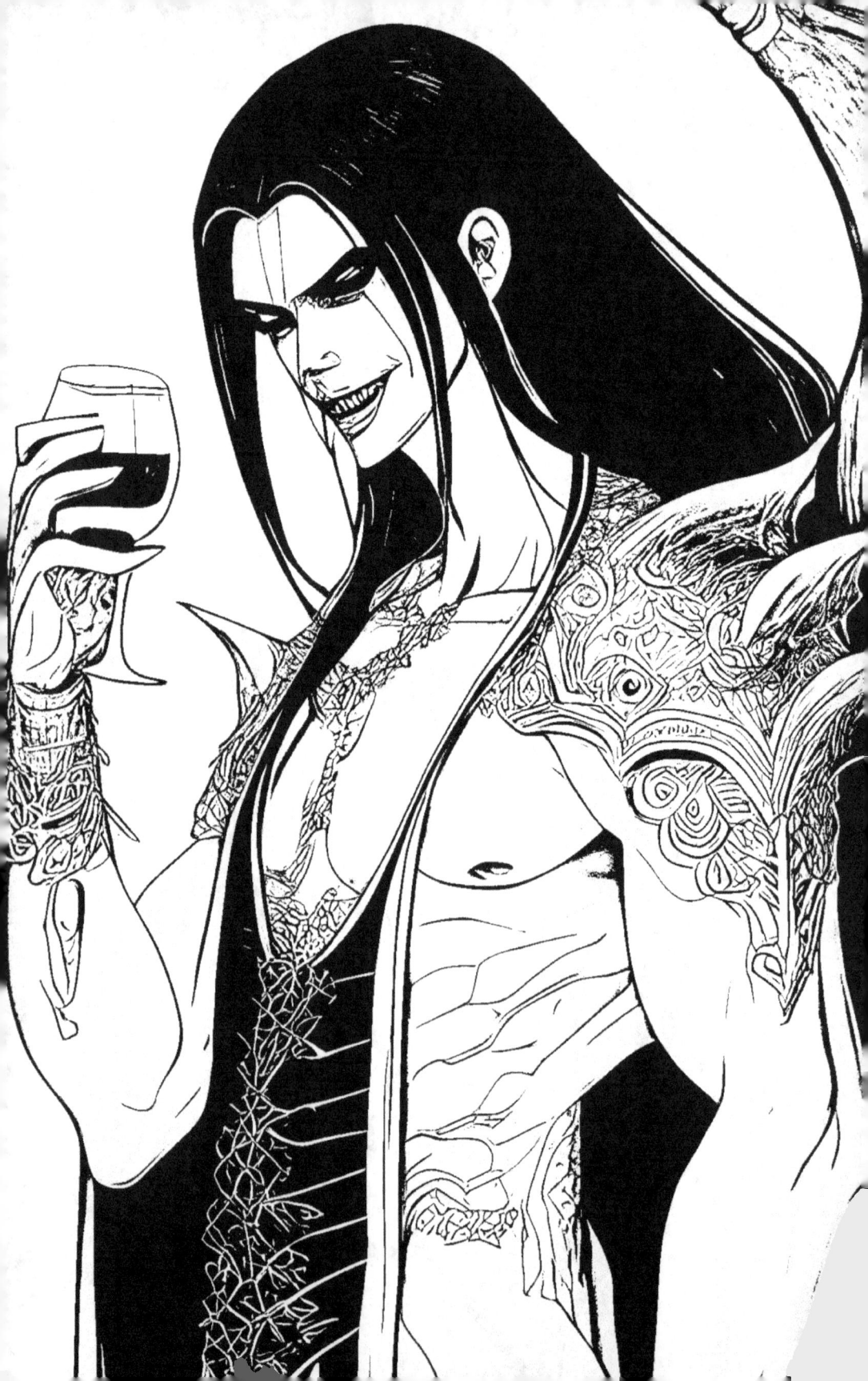

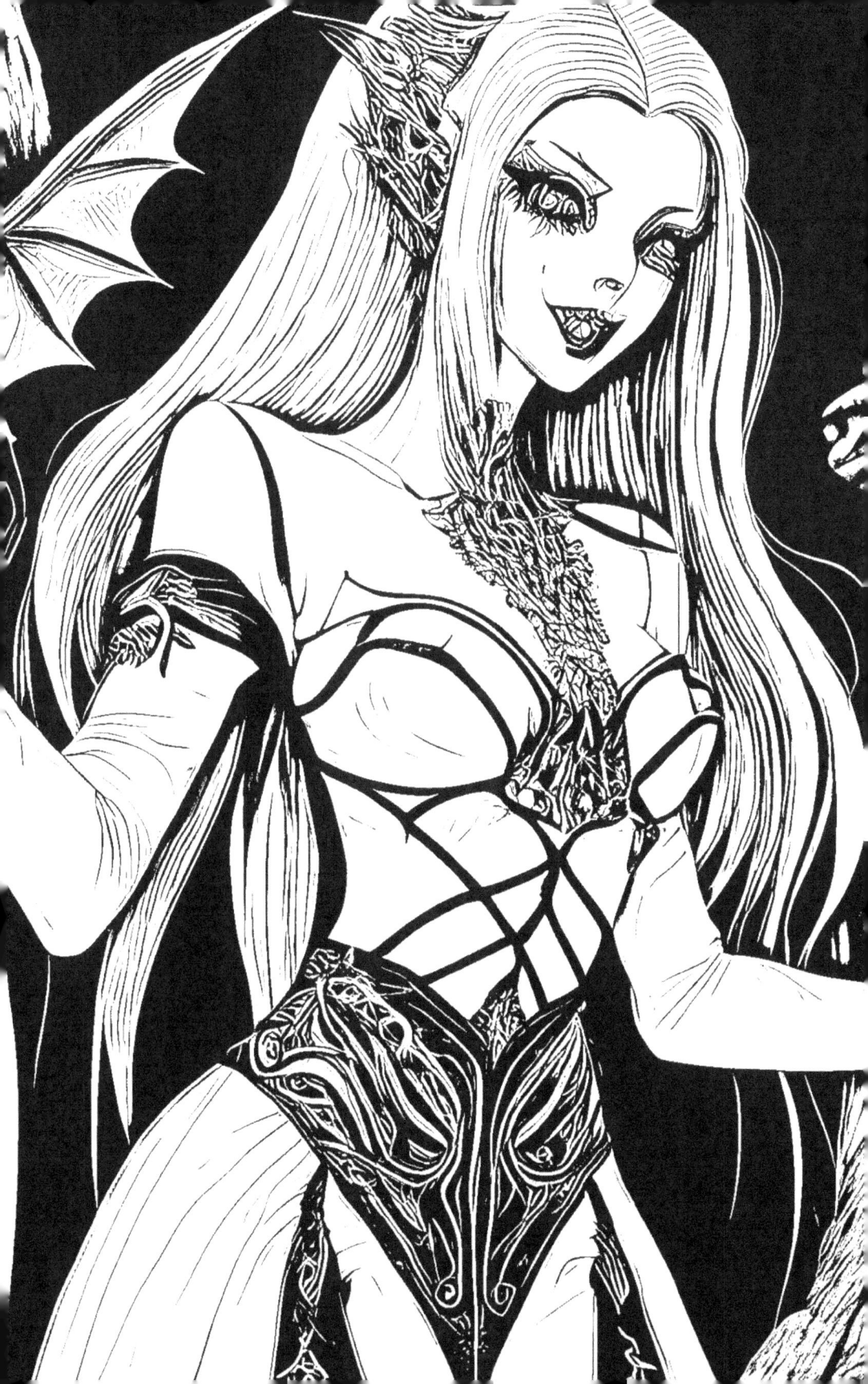

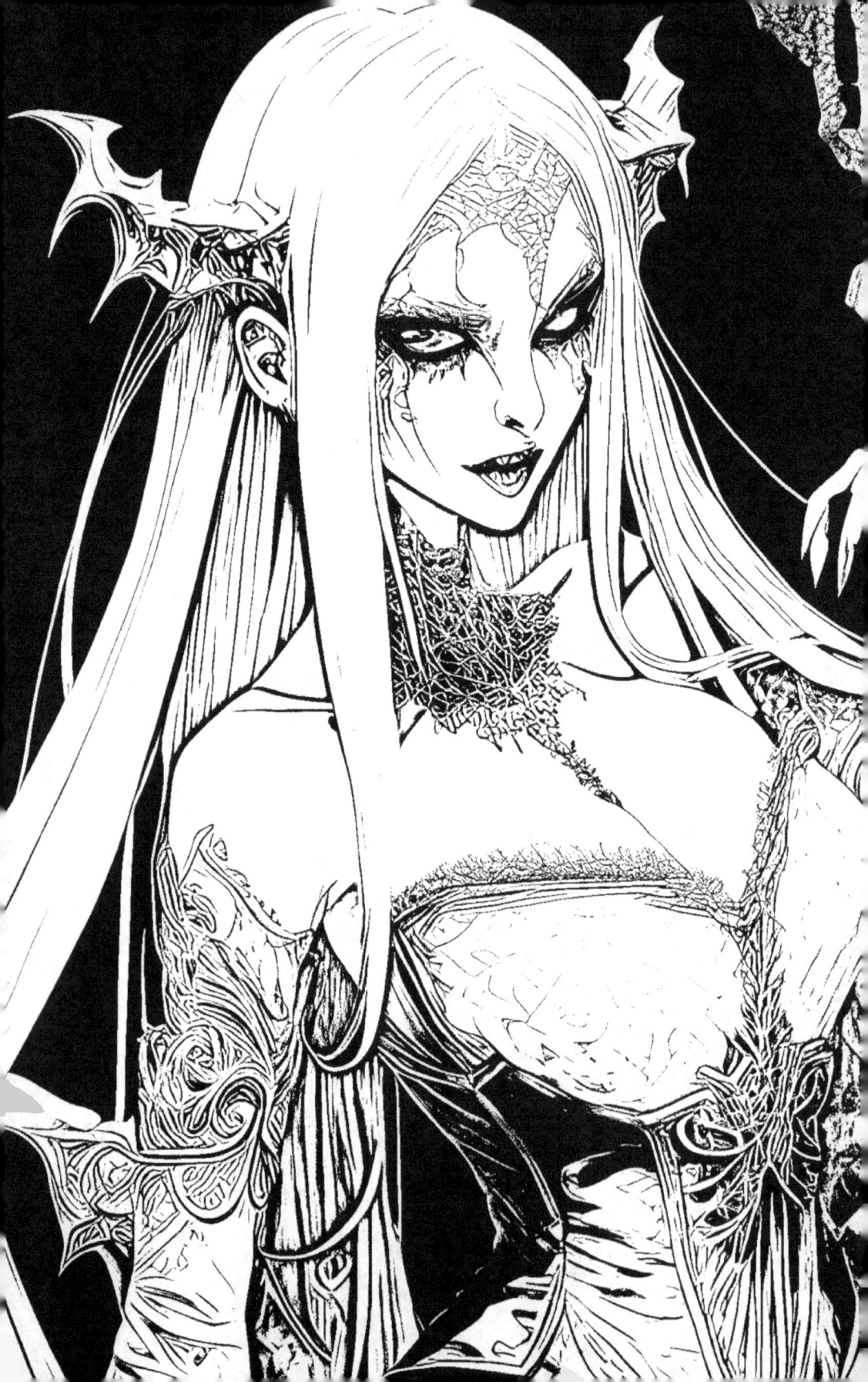

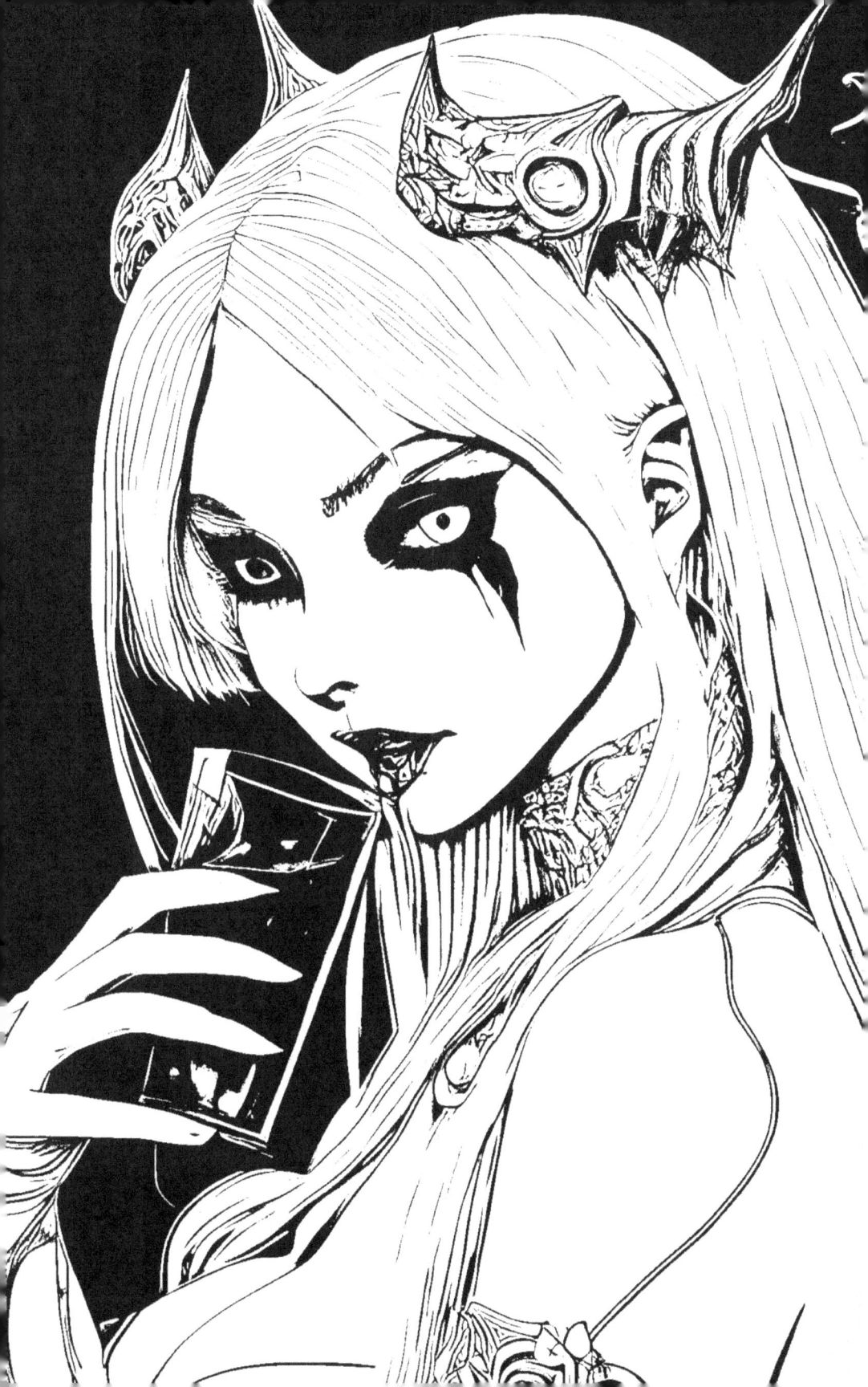

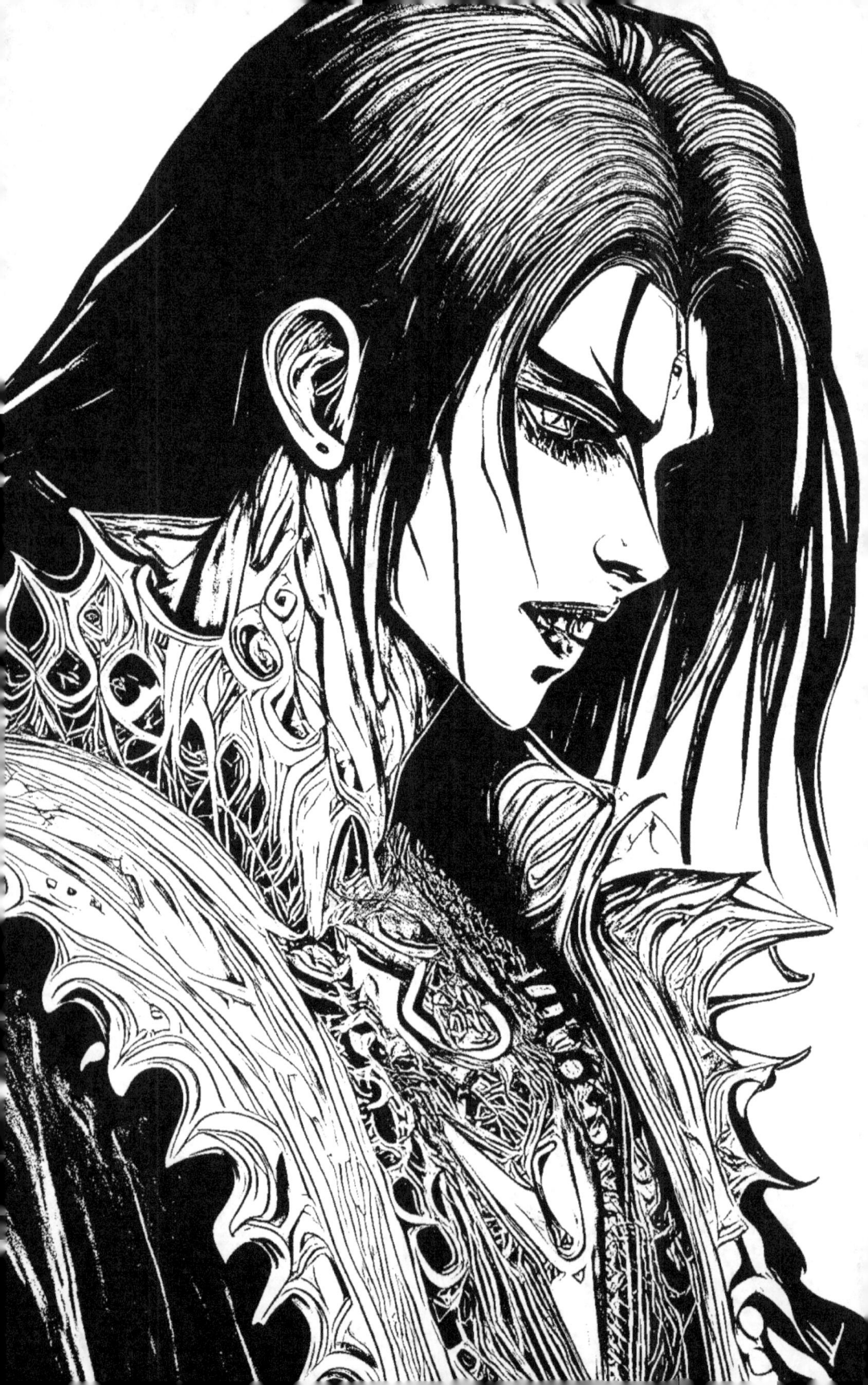

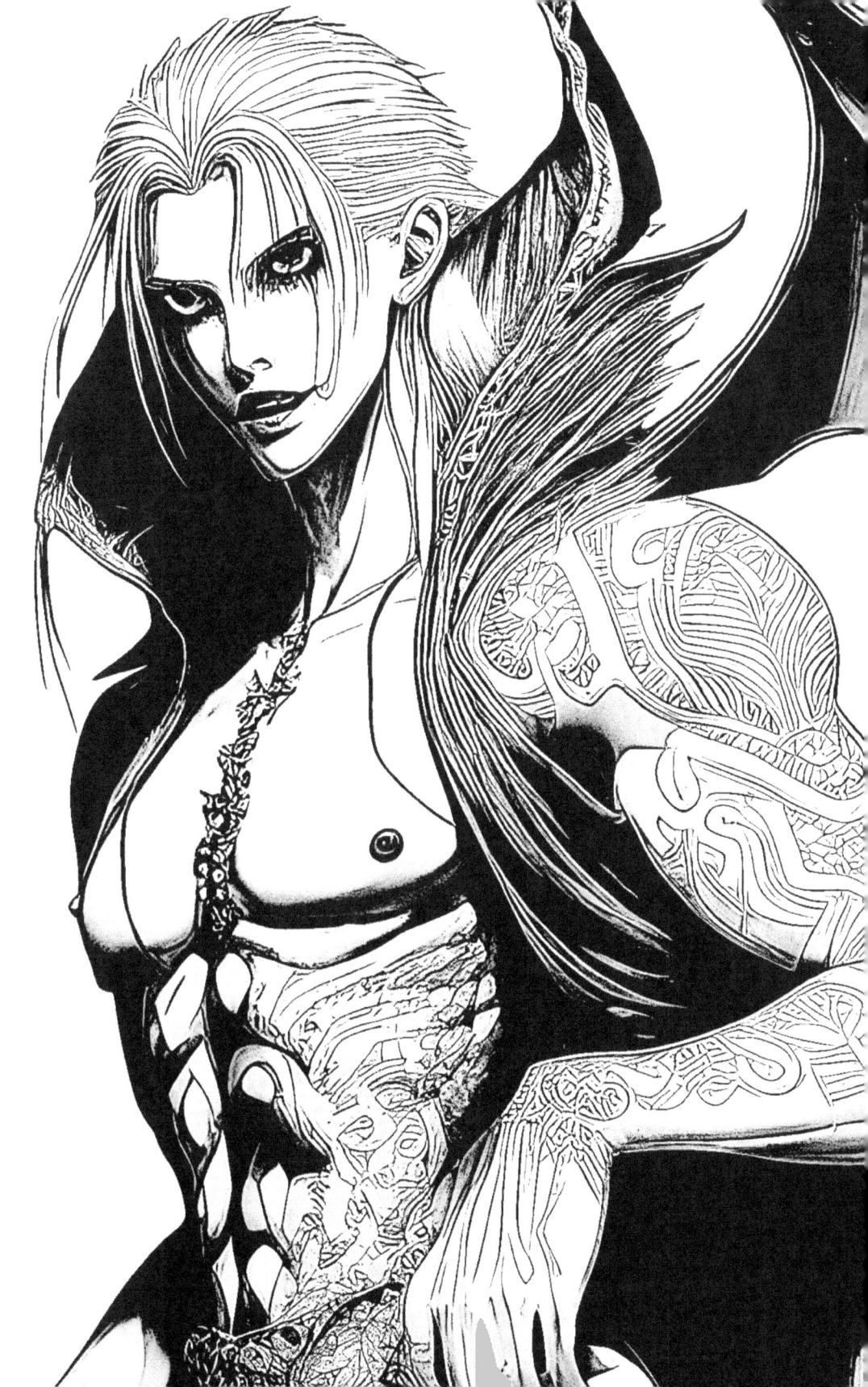

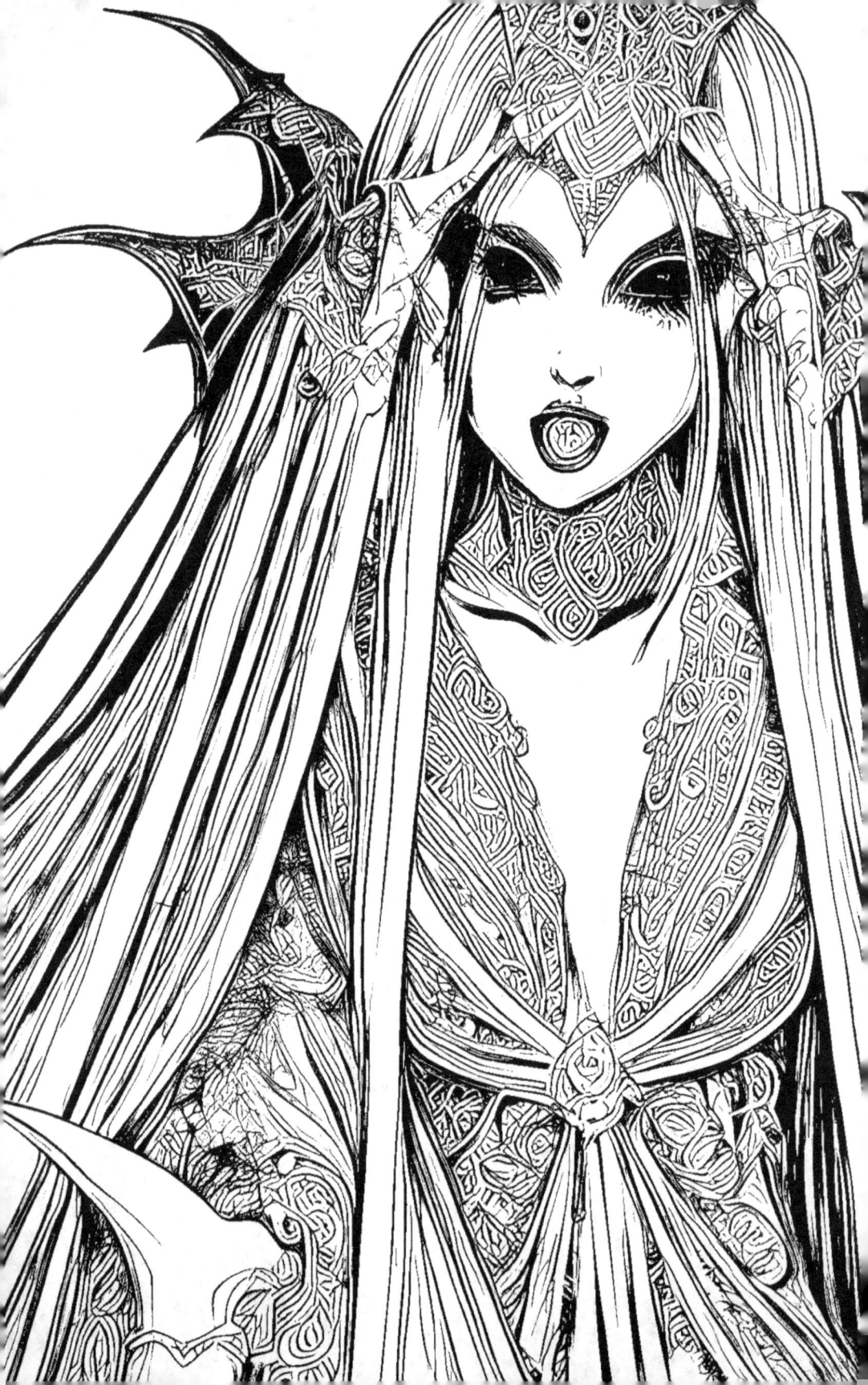

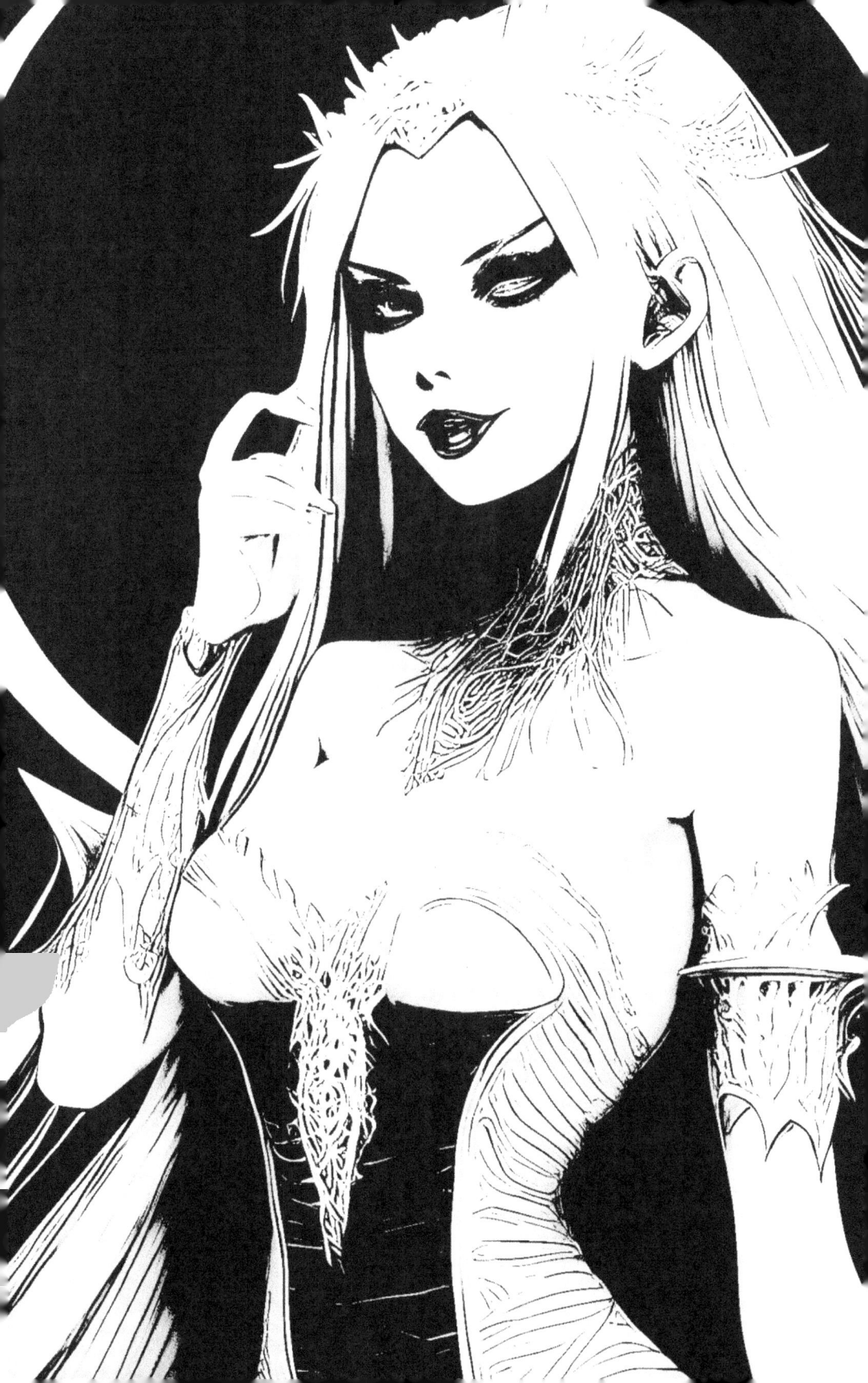

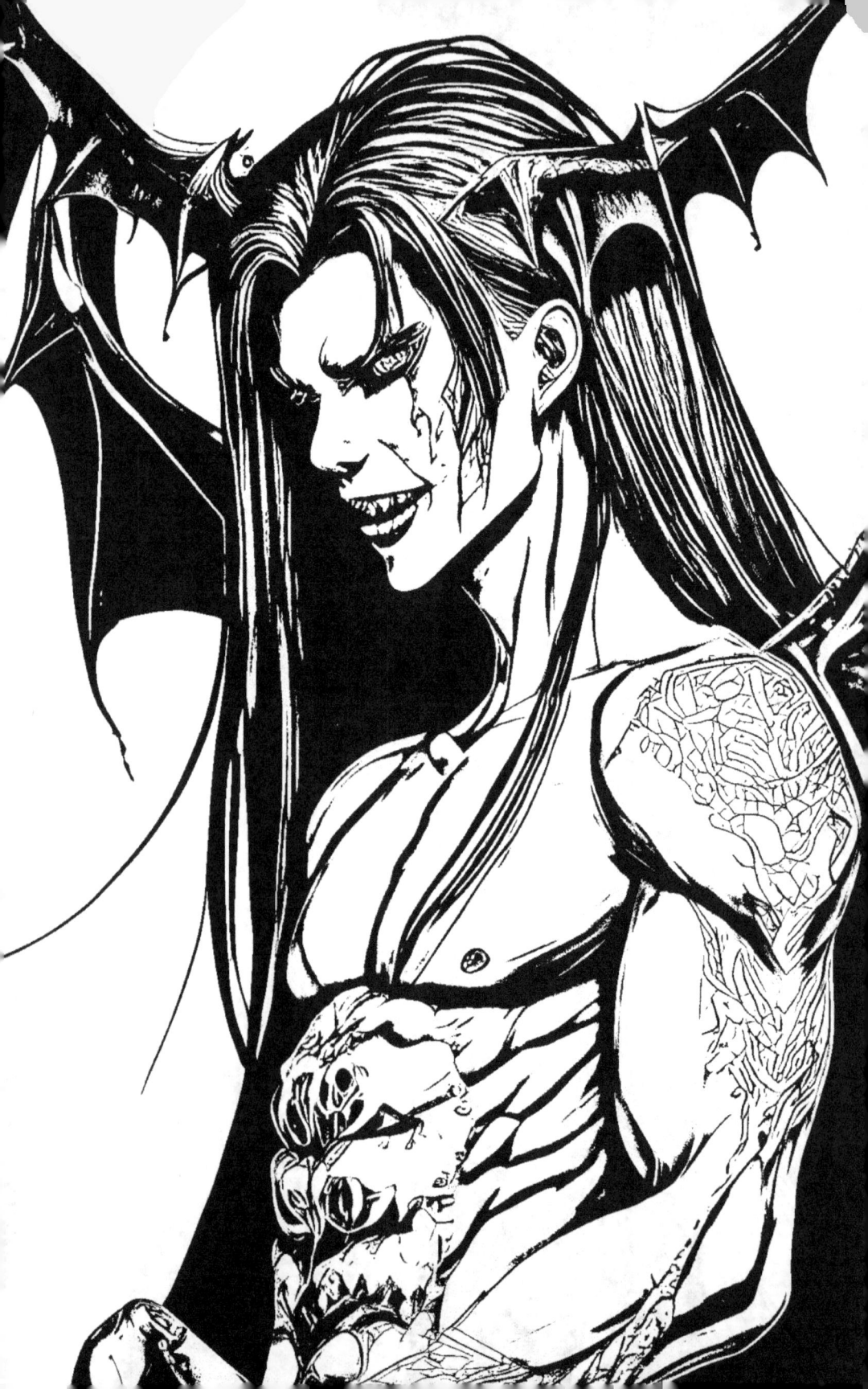

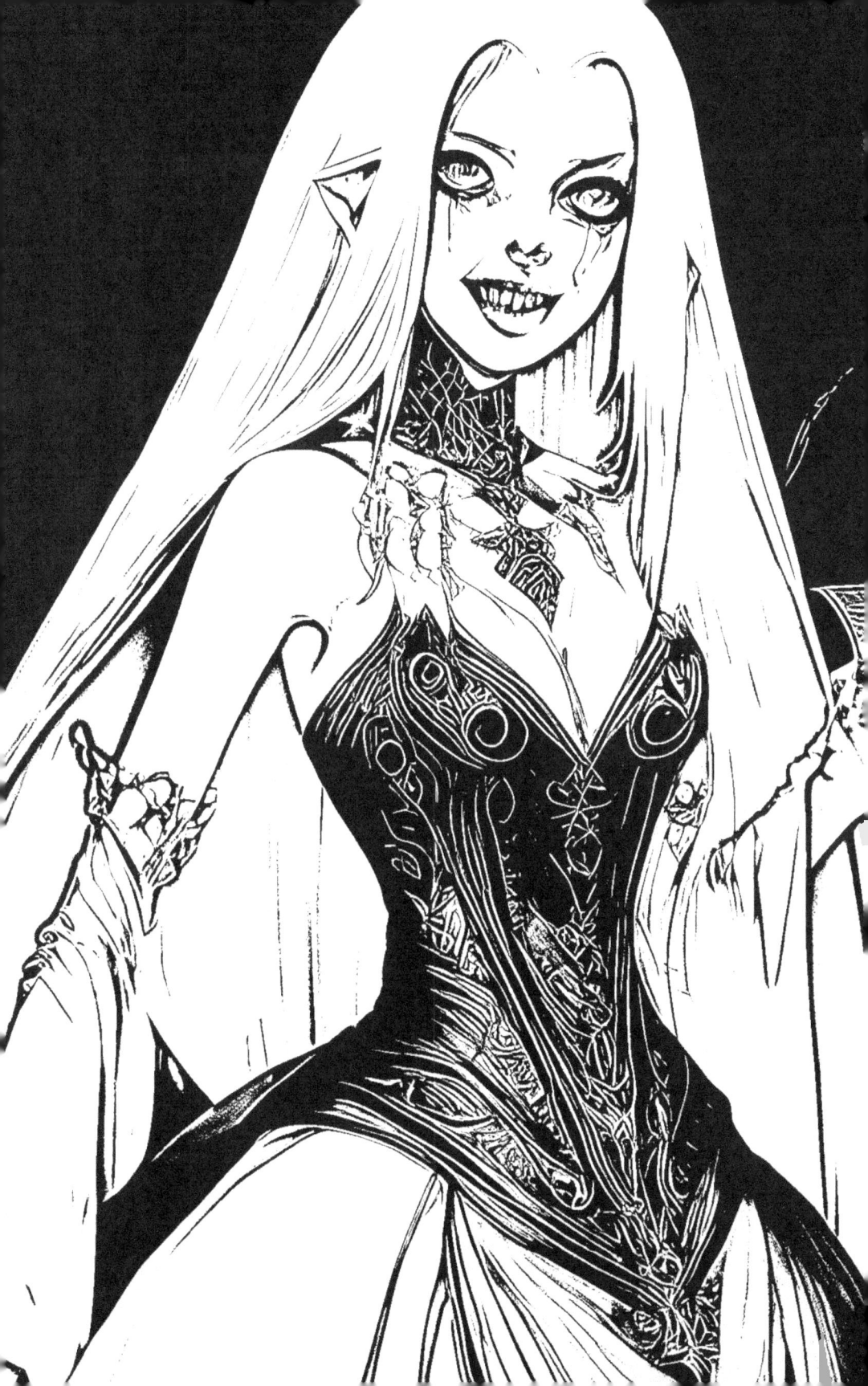

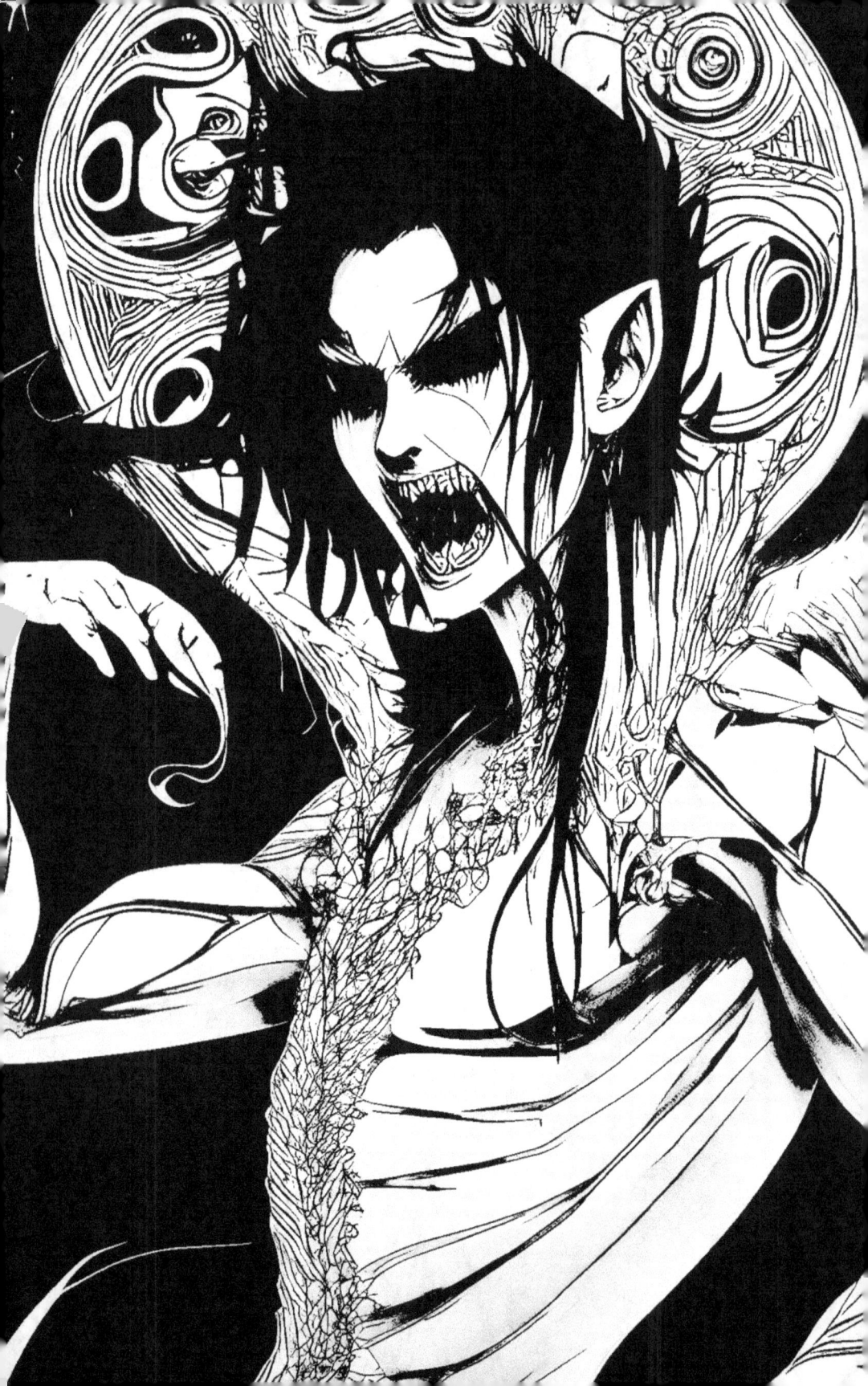

jeremyburt@ishopdailyonline.com jburt_01@hotmail.com
Make Money Online: https://ishopdailyonline.com
Print On Demand: https://ishopdaily.redbubble.com
Print On Demand @ Etsy: https://ishopdailyonline.etsy.com
dj12mind Instrumental Music Albums: https://dj12mind.com
Affiliate Products: https://index.ishopdailyonline.com
Patreon: https://www.patreon.com/user?u=80194438
Facebook: https://www.facebook.com/jeremy.burt2
Youtube:
https://www.youtube.com/channel/UCwV3nApPDh3dNHUGIX4w5nA
tiktok: https://www.tiktok.com/@jeremyburt4?lang=en
amazon: https://www.amazon.com/author/jeremyburt
THANK YOU FOR CHECKING IT OUT!

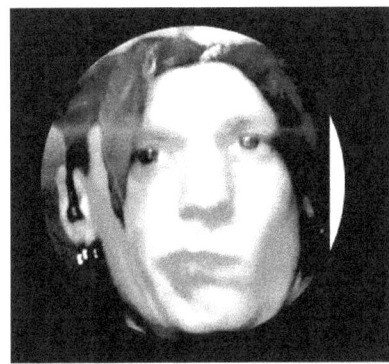

www.ingramcontent.com/pod-product-compliance
Lightning Source LLC
Chambersburg PA
CBHW072236230526
45466CB00024B/2076